Survival Summary
Part One

Important Words

yes	ja	*yah*
no	nein	*nine*
please	bitte	*bit-eh*
thank you	danke	*dahnk-eh*
excuse me	Entschuldi-gung	*ent-shool-dig-ung*
hello (day)	Guten Tag	*goo-ten tahk*
hello (evening)	Guten Abend	*goo-ten ah-bent*
hello (Austria)	Grüß Gott	*gRews got*
goodbye	Auf Wieder-sehen	*owf vee-deh(r)-zayn*
and	und	*unt*
or	oder	*oh-deh(r)*
not	nicht	*ni^{ch}t*
only	nur	*noo(r)*
also, too	auch	*ow$_{ch}$*
day	der Tag	*day(r) tahk*
week	die Woche	*dee voh$_{ch}$-eh*
morning	der Vormittag	*day(r) foh(r)-mit-tahk*
afternoon	der Nachmittag	*nah$_{ch}$-mit-tahk*
evening	der Abend	*day(r) ah-bent*
night	die Nacht	*dee nah$_{ch}$t*
yesterday	gestern	*ges-teh(r)n*
today	heute	*hoy-teh*
tomorrow	morgen	*mo(r)-gen*
here	hier	*hee(r)*
there	da	*dah*

Question Words

where?	wo?	*voh?*
where from?	wovon?	*voh-fon?*
what?	was?	*vahs?*
when?	wann?	*vahn?*
how?	wie?	*vee?*
how long?	wie lange?	*vee lahng-eh?*
how much?	wieviel?	*vee-feel?*
how many?	wie viele?	*vee feel-eh?*
why?	warum?	*vah-Room?*
who?	wer?	*vay(r)?*

Useful Words

big	groß	*gRohs*
small	klein	*kline*
a lot	viel	*feel*
a little	ein bißchen	*ine bis-^{ch}en*
hot	heiß	*hice*
cold	kalt	*kahlt*
good/well	gut	*goot*
bad	schlecht	*shle^{ch}t*
enough	genug	*geh-nook*

Emergencies

Help!	Hilfe!	*hilf-eh!*
Stop!	Halt!	*hahlt!*
Watch out!	Vorsicht!	*foh(r)-zi^{ch}t!*
Go away!	Gehen Sie weg!	*gay-en zee vek!*
Fire!	Feuer!	*foy-eh(r)!*
Call __!	Rufen Sie __!	*Roof-en zee __!*
a doctor	einen Arzt	*ine-en ah(r)tst*
an ambulance	einen Kran-kenwagen	*ine-en kRahnk-en-vah-gen*
the police	die Polizei	*dee poh-li-tsy*
It hurts here.	Es tut hier weh.	*es toot hee(r) vay*

Useful Phrases

What is that?	Was ist das?	*vahs ist dahs?*
That is __.	Das ist __.	*dahs ist __*
Where is __?	Wo ist __?	*voh ist __?*
When is __?	Wann ist __?	*vahn ist __?*
Can you __?	Können Sie __?	*ker-nen zee __?*
Do you have?	Haben Sie __?	*hah-ben zee __?*
I have __.	Ich habe __.	*i^{ch} hah-beh __*
I would like __.	Ich möchte __.	*i^{ch} mer^{ch}-teh __*
I'm looking for __.	Ich suche __.	*i^{ch} zoo-$_{ch}$eh __*
I need __.	Ich brauche _	*i^{ch} bRow-$_{ch}$eh __*
How much does that cost?	Wieviel kostet das?	*vee-feel kost-et dahs?*
I'll take it.	Ich nehme es.	*i^{ch} nay-meh es*
Just a moment.	Einen Mo-ment.	*ine-en moh-ment*
Do you speak English?	Sprechen Sie Englisch?	*shpRe^{ch}-en zee eng-lish?*
I don't understand.	Ich verstehe nicht.	*i^{ch} feh(r)-shtay-eh ni^{ch}t*

Directions

left	links	*links*
right	rechts	*Re^{ch}ts*
straight	geradeaus	*geh-Rah-deh-ows*
keep going straight	immer gerade-aus	*im-eh(r) geh-Rah-deh-ows*
to the north	nördlich	*nerd-li^{ch}*
to the south	südlich	*zewd-li^{ch}*
to the east	östlich	*erst-li^{ch}*
to the west	westlich	*vest-li^{ch}*
nearby	in der Nähe	*in day(r) nay-eh*
far (away)	weit (weg)	*vite (vek)*
up	hinauf	*hin-owf*
down	hinunter	*hin-un-teh(r)*
Go __.	Gehen Sie __.	*gay-en zee __*

Sightseeing

Where is __?	Wo ist __?	voh ist __?
bridge	die Brücke	dee bRew-keh
castle	die Burg	dee boo(r)k
	das Schloß	dahs shlos
cathedral	der Dom	day(r) dohm
checkroom	die Garderobe	dee gah(r)-deh-Roh-beh
church	die Kirche	dee kee(r)-ch eh
garden	der Garten	day(r) gah(r)-ten
museum	das Museum	dahs mu-zay-um
palace	das Schloß	dahs shlos
	der Palast	day(r) pah-lahst
park	der Park	day(r) pah(r)k
square	der Platz	day(r) plahts
ticket	die Karte	dee kah(r)-teh
for two	für zwei	few(r) tsvy
information	die Auskunft	dee ows-kunft
town center	das Zentrum	dahs tsen-tRum

Days and Times

Monday	Montag	mohn-tahk
Tuesday	Dienstag	deens-tahk
Wednesday	Mittwoch	mit-vo ch
Thursday	Donnerstag	don-eh(r)s-tahk
Friday	Freitag	fRy-tahk
Saturday	Samstag	zahms-tahk
Sunday	Sonntag	zon-tahk
minute	die Minute	dee mi-noo-teh
hour	die Stunde	dee shtun-deh
day	der Tag	day(r) tahk
week	die Woche	dee vo ch-eh
month	der Monat	day(r) moh-naht

Lodging

hotel	das Hotel	dahs hoh-tel
guesthouse	die Pension	dee pens-yohn
reservation	die Reservier-ung	dee Reh-zeh(r)-veeR-ung
room	das Zimmer	dahs tsim-eh(r)
Do you have rooms available?	Haben Sie Zimmer frei?	hah-ben zee tsim-eh(r) fRei?
How much does __ cost?	Wieviel kostet __?	vee-feel kos-tet __?
a double room	ein Doppel-zimmer	ine dop-el tsim-eh(r)
a single room	ein Einzel-zimmer	ine ine-tsel-tsim-eh(r)
with shower	mit Dusche	mit doo-sheh
with bath	mit Bad	mit baht
with breakfast	mit Frühstück	mit fRew-shtewk
for one night	für eine Nacht	few(r) ine-eh nah ch t
for __ nights	für __ Nächte	few(r) __ ne ch -teh
from . . . to	von . . . bis	fon. . . bis

Shopping

How much does it cost?	Wieviel kostet das?	vee-feel kos-tet dahs?
I would like _	Ich möchte _	i ch me ch -teh __
I'm looking for __.	Ich suche __.	i ch zoo ch -eh __
Do you have __?	Haben Sie __?	hah-ben zee __?
Where is ___?	Wo ist __?	voh ist __?
Where are __?	Wo sind __?	voh zint __?
Do you take credit cards?	Nehmen Sie Kreditkarten?	nay-men zee kReh-deet-kah(r)-ten?
that	das	dahs
here	hier	hee(r)
cash register	die Kasse	dee kah-seh
checkout	die Kasse	dee kah-seh
That's all.	Das ist alles.	dahs ist ahl-es
receipt	die Quittung	dee kvit-ung
I'm just looking.	Ich schaue nur.	i ch shau-eh noo(r)
I'll take it.	Ich nehme es.	i ch nay-meh es
open	geöffnet	geh-erf-net
closed	geschlossen	geh-shlos-en
tobacconist's shop	die Tabak-handlung	dee tah-bahk-hahnt-lung
bookstore	die Buch-handlung	dee boo ch -hahnt-lung
department store	das Kaufhaus	dahs kowf-hows
market	der Markt	day(r) mah(r)kt
supermarket	der Super-markt	day(r) zoo-peh(r)-mah(r)kt
bakery	die Bäckerei	dee bek-eh-Rye
pastry shop	die Konditorei	dee kon-dee-tor-Rye
butcher shop	die Fleischerei	dee fly-sheh-Rye
pharmacy	die Apotheke	dee ah-poh-tay-keh
flower shop	das Blumen-geschäft	dahs bloo-men-geh-sheft
hair stylist	die Friseuse	dee fRi-zew-zeh
camera shop	das Foto-geschäft	dahs foh-toh-geh-sheft

Colors

black	schwarz	shvah(r)ts
blue	blau	blau
brown	braun	bRown
gray	grau	gRau
green	grün	gRewn
pink	rosa	Roh-zah
purple	violett	vee-oh-let
red	rot	Roht
white	weiß	vice
yellow	gelb	gelp
dark __	dunkel __	dunk-el __
light __	hell __	hel __

Survival Summary
Part Two

Transportation

taxi	das Taxi	*dahs <u>tahk</u>-see*
to __	zu __	*tsoo*
I stop here.	Ich halte hier.	*i^{ch} <u>hahl</u>-teh hee(r)*
bus	der Bus	*day(r) boos*
entrance	der Eingang	*day(r) <u>ine</u>-gahng*
exit	der Ausgang	*day(r) <u>ows</u>-gahng*
subway	die U-Bahn	*dee <u>oo</u>-bahn*
train	der Zug	*day(r) tsook*
train station	der Bahnhof	*day(r) <u>bahn</u>-hof*
ticket	die Fahrkarte	*dee <u>fah(r)</u>-kah(r)-teh*
car	das Auto	*dahs <u>ow</u>-toh*
I would like to rent a car.	Ich möchte ein Auto mieten.	*i^{ch} <u>me</u>f^{ch}-teh ine <u>ow</u>-toh <u>mee</u>-ten*
I have a reservation.	Ich habe eine Reservierung	*i^{ch} <u>hah</u>-beh <u>ine</u>-eh Reh-zeh(r)-<u>vee</u>R-ung*
from . . . to	von . . . bis	*fon . . . bis*
driver's license	der Führer-schein	*day(r) <u>fewR</u>-eh(r)-shine*
plane flight	der Flug	*day(r) flook*
airport	der Flughafen	*day(r) <u>flook</u>-hah-fen*
information	die Auskunft	*dee <u>ows</u>-kunft*

Services

bathroom	die Toilette	*dee toy-<u>let</u>-eh*
gentlemen	Herren	*<u>heh</u>-Ren*
ladies	Damen	*<u>dah</u>-men*
available	frei	*fRy*
occupied	besetzt	*beh-<u>zetst</u>*
ATM	der Geldauto-mat	*day(r) <u>gelt</u>-ow-toh-maht*
bank	die Bank	*dee bahnk*
cell phone	das Handy	*dahs <u>hen</u>-dee*
telephone	das Telefon	*dahs <u>tay</u>-leh-fone*
post office	die Post	*dee post*
stamps	Briefmarken	*<u>bReef</u>-mah(r)-ken*
to America	nach Amerika	*nah_{ch} ah-<u>may</u>-Ree-kah*
by airmail	per Luftpost	*pehr <u>luft</u>-post*

Temperature Conversion Guide

1. Multiply the Celsius reading by 2.
2. Add 30, for approximate Fahrenheit temperature.

Numbers

0	null	*nul*
1	eins	*ines*
2	zwei	*tsvy*
3	drei	*dRy*
4	vier	*fee(r)*
5	fünf	*fewnf*
6	sechs	*ze^{ch}s*
7	sieben	*<u>zee</u>-ben*
8	acht	*ah_{ch}t*
9	neun	*noyn*
10	zehn	*tsayn*
11	elf	*elf*
12	zwölf	*tsverlf*
13	dreizehn	*<u>dRy</u>-tsayn*
14	vierzehn	*<u>fee(r)</u>-tsayn*
15	fünfzehn	*<u>fewnf</u>-tsayn*
16	sechzehn	*<u>ze^{ch}</u>-tsayn*
17	siebzehn	*<u>zeep</u>-tsayn*
18	achtzehn	*<u>ah_{ch}t</u>-tsayn*
19	neunzehn	*<u>noyn</u>-tsayn*
20	zwanzig	*<u>tsvahn</u>-tsi^{ch}*
21	einundzwanzig	*<u>ine</u>-unt-tsvahn-tsi^{ch}*
22	zweiundzwan-zig	*<u>tsvy</u>-unt-tsvahn-tsi^{ch}*
33	dreiunddreißig	*<u>dRy</u>-unt-dRy -si^{ch}*
44	vierundvierzig	*<u>fee(r)</u>-unt-fee(r)-tsi^{ch}*
55	fünfundfünfzig	*<u>fewnf</u>-unt-fewnf-tsi^{ch}*
66	sechsundsech-zig	*<u>zechs</u>-unt-zech-tsi^{ch}*
77	siebenundsieb-zig	*<u>zee</u>-ben-unt-zeep-tsi^{ch}*
88	achtundachtzig	*<u>ah_{ch}t</u>-unt-ah_{ch}t-tsi^{ch}*
99	neunundneun-zig	*<u>noyn</u>-unt-noyn-tsi^{ch}*
100	(ein)hundert	*(ine)<u>hun</u>-deh(r)t*
101	hunderteins	*hun-deh(r)t-<u>ines</u>*
102	hundertzwei	*hun-deh(r)t-<u>tsvy</u>*
200	zweihundert	*<u>tsvy</u>-hun-deh(r)t*
300	dreihundert	*<u>dRy</u>-hun-deh(r)t*
400	vierhundert	*<u>fee(r)</u>-hun-deh(r)t*
500	fünfhundert	*<u>fewnf</u>-hun-deh(r)t*
600	sechshundert	*<u>ze^{ch}s</u>-hun-deh(r)t*
700	siebenhundert	*<u>zee</u>-ben-hun-deh(r)t*
800	achthundert	*<u>ah_{ch}t</u>-hun-deh(r)t*
900	neunhundert	*<u>noyn</u>-hun-deh(r)t*
1.000	(ein)tausend	*(ine)<u>tow</u>-zent*
2.000	zweitausend	*<u>tsvy</u>-tow-zent*
40.000	vierzigtausend	*<u>feer</u>-tsi^{ch}-tow-zent*

Eating Out

Excuse me!	Entschuldigung!	ent-_shool_-dig-ung!
I would like __	Ich möchte __	i^{ch} _mer_^{ch}-teh __
Can you recommend?	Können Sie _ empfehlen?	_ker_-nen zee __ emp-_fay_-len?
something	etwas	_et_-vahs
a red/white wine	einen roten/ weißen Wein	_ine_-en _Rot_-en/ _vy_-sen vine
Enjoy your meal!	Guten Appetit!	_goo_-ten ah-peh-_teet_!
Check, please!	Zahlen, bitte!	_tsah_-len, _bit_-eh
It tastes good.	Es schmekt.	es shmekt
I need __.	Ich brauche _	i^{ch} _bRow_-_{ch}eh _
the menu	die Speisekarte	dee _shpy_-zeh-kah(r)-teh
the set menu	das Menü	dahs meh-_new_
the wine list	die Weinkarte	dee _vine_-kah(r)-teh
a glass	ein Glas	ine glahs
a bottle	eine Flasche	_ine_-eh _flah_-sheh
a plate	ein(en) Teller	_ine_-(en) _tel_-eh(r)
a fork	eine Gabel	_ine_-eh _gah_-bel
a spoon	ein(en) Löffel	_ine_-(en) _ler_-fel
a knive	ein Messer	ine _mes_-eh(r)
a napkin	eine Serviette	_ine_-eh zeh(r)-vee-_et_-eh
breakfast	das Frühstück	dahs _fRew_-shtewk
lunch	das Mittagessen	dahs _mit_-tahk-es-en
supper	das Abendessen	dahs _ah_-bent-es-en

Reading the Menu

Check the dictionaries for more terms and for pronunciations.

Apfel	apple	Hendl	chicken	Reh	venison
Apfelsine	orange	Himbeeren	raspberries	Reis	rice
Bauern-schmaus	hearty meat platter	Honig	honey	Rindfleisch	beef
		Huhn	chicken	Rostbraten	rump steak
Bier	beer	Kaffee	coffee	rot	red
Birne	pear	Kalbfleisch	veal	Rouladen	beef roll
Bohnen	beans	Kaninchen	rabbit	Saft	juice
Brot	bread	Kartoffel	potato	Sahne	cream
Brötchen	roll(s)	Käse	cheese	Salat	salad, lettuce
Ei(er)	egg(s)	Kirschen	cherries	Salz	salt
Eis	ice cream	Kloß/Klöße	dumpling(s)	Schlag__	whipped __
Ente	duck	Knödel	dumpling(s)	Schweine-fleisch	pork
Erbsen	peas	Kohl	cabbage		
Erdapfel	potato	Kohlensäure	carbonation	Semmel	roll
Erdbeeren	strawberries	Kraut	cabbage	Senf	mustard
Erdnüsse	peanuts	Kuchen	cake	scharf	spicy
Essig	vinegar	Lamm	lamb	Schinken	ham
Fleisch	meat	Leber	liver	Soße	sauce
Forelle	trout	Mandeln	almonds	Spargel	asparagus
Frikadellen	meat patties	Marmelade	jam	Speck	bacon
Gans	goose	Meeresfrüchte	seafood	Spinat	spinach
Gebäck	pastries	Milch	milk	still	non-fizzy
gebacken	baked	Mineral-wasser	mineral water	Suppe	soup
gebraten	fried	Nachspeisen	desserts	Tagesmenü	daily special
Geflügel	poultry	Nachtisch	dessert	Thunfisch	tuna
gefüllt	filled	Nudeln	noodles	Trauben	grapes
gemischt	mixed	Nüsse	nuts	Truthahn	turkey
Gemüse	vegetables	Obst	fruit	Vorspeisen	appetizers
Getränke	drinks	Paradeiser	tomato	weiß	white
grüner Salat	lettuce	Pfeffer	pepper	Wiener Schnitzel	breaded veal cutlet
Gurke	cucumber	Pfirsich	peach	Wild	game
Hähnchen	chicken	Pilze	mushrooms	Wurst	sausage
Haselnüsse	hazelnuts	Pommes frites	French fries	Zitrone	lemon
Heidelbeeren	blueberries	Rahm	cream	Zucker	sugar
heiße Schokolade	hot chocolate			Zwiebel	onion

German Survival Guide

**The Language and Culture You Need
to Travel with Confidence
in Germany and Austria**

(Expanded Version)

Elizabeth Bingham, Ph.D.

World Prospect Press
Waverly, Iowa

Publisher's Note

This book is designed to help prepare travelers for their trips abroad. Its purpose is to educate and entertain. It is sold with the understanding that the publisher and author are not giving legal or financial advice. The author and World Prospect Press shall have neither liability nor responsibility to any person or entity with respect to any loss or damage caused, or alleged to be caused, directly or indirectly, by the information contained in this book.

World Prospect Press
P.O. Box 253
Waverly, IA 50677
www.worldprospect.com

Second Edition Revised (Expanded Version), 2015

Publisher's Cataloging-in-Publication
Bingham, Elizabeth.
    German survival guide : the language and culture you need to travel with confidence in Germany and Austria / Elizabeth Bingham. – 2nd ed., rev.
    p. cm.
    Rev. ed. of : German survival guide : the language and culture you need to travel with confidence in Germany and Austria. c2001.
    Includes bibliographical references and index.
    LCCN: 2007939868
    ISBN: 978-0-9703734-6-5

    1. German language—Conversation and phrase books—English. 2. German language—Study and teaching (Continuing education)—English speakers. 3. Germany—Social life and customs—21st century. 4. Austria—Social life and customs—21st century. I. Title.

PF3121.B56 2008   438.2'421

Table of Contents

Acknowledgments

It's a sobering task to think back on how this book developed and realize how indebted I am to so many people. This edition would not have happened without the varied and vital contributions of the following individuals.

For native insights into German and Austrian culture, I thank Heidi and Mirjam Aßmann, my German "mother" Inge and her partner, Dorothee Weymann, Claudia Woelk, Ronald Kirschner, Irene and Manfred Woelk, Friedrich Synder, Elvira and Reinhard Holzer, Christoph and Charlie Holzer, Leo and Jutta Ratschbacher, Eveline Ganglmair, Günter Scherfler, Uta Synder, Ursula Hoegsberg, and Hans Kloibhofer. They have greatly enriched my travels and this book by sharing their intimate cultural knowledge.

For their personal travel observations, I thank David Zelle, Emily Bingham, Dr. Lynn Olson, Terry Letsche, Julie Breutzmann, Don and Fannie Albrecht, Don and Ursula Hoegsberg, Beverly Moffitt, and Linda Bingham. Their many comments and questions were invaluable in deciding what travelers need or want to know.

For manuscript proofreading, I am deeply grateful to David Zelle, Elaina Toenjes and Ursula Hoegsberg. Their sharp eyes and gentle pens saved me many printed mistakes. Any errors that crept in are entirely my own responsibility.

For library cataloging guidance, I thank Pam Madden, Randall Schroeder, Margaret Hubbard, and Jean Byl for sharing their professional knowledge. They helped untangle the mysteries of the cataloging data block and got this book to press a bit sooner than otherwise would have happened.

On the printing end, I am grateful to Deborrah Shankleton and Bill Wearne for their expert knowledge and patient guidance. For technical assistance and unflagging encouragement, I thank John Zelle, who always finds the time to help me, even when he doesn't have it. This book would not be possible without him.

Acknowledgments for the 1st edition

As is usually the case, many people contributed to the development of this book, either directly or indirectly. I wish to thank Lynn and Margaret Poppen, Vern and Jean Byl, and Marie Zelle for being the initial "guinea pigs" for this material. I also thank Jan Nelson, who prodded me to develop the course from which this book grew.

I owe great thanks to the people who critiqued early versions of the manuscript: Elaina Toenjes, Linda Bingham, Ed Deuhr, Beverly Moffitt, Steve Maricle, and Jessica Struck. Thank you, especially, to Jean Byl for her in-depth consultation. The input from these readers was invaluable in shaping this book.

For Austrian and German cultural insights, I relied on Eveline Ganglmair, Irene and Manfred Woelk, and special friends around Berlin, who were all generous with their time and their knowledge. I owe a special debt to Dorothee Weymann, who volunteered her professional editing skills on her personal time and contributed much fine-tuning to a late version of this book.

On the production end, I thank Tami DeFant for her knowledge of printing and her amazing attentiveness; Dustin Schadt for his initiative and inventiveness in packaging; and George Foster for his striking cover design and seemingly endless patience.

Looking back a bit farther, I would like to thank Gordon Hoffert, who started me on the path to German proficiency many years ago; Dr. Jürgen Koppensteiner, who shared his love of Austria and taught me much about the land and its language; and Dr. Frank Donahue, who trained me in foreign language pedagogy. They're the best, and I was privileged to be taught and influenced by them.

Finally, I want to thank my family for their unwavering support and their willingness to put up with ever more chaos in our household. We have learned that the family that writes together, well, has a very messy house. . . .

About the Author

Elizabeth Bingham loves to travel and loves to teach. She combines these passions in her *Survival Guide* series, in which she prepares travelers for the language and culture they will experience abroad.

As an avid traveler, Dr. Bingham knows how useful even a little cultural knowledge and language ability are. She, too, has been in an unfamiliar country, bewildered by the foreign culture and unable to communicate. Her *Survival Guides* grew out of her desire to help others avoid that situation, to help them know what to expect, what to do, and what to say when they visit a different country. She has found that even minimal preparation can make a world of difference in the enjoyment and rewards of a trip abroad.

Dr. Bingham has a Ph.D. in Applied Linguistics/Foreign Language Education from the University of Texas at Austin. She has taught writing and German at the university level. In addition to extensive European travel, she has lived in Germany and Austria, teaching English and conducting research there. Since 1999, she has lived in northeast Iowa, promoting foreign language and culture through teaching and writing.

Dr. Bingham can be contacted by e-mail through World Prospect Press at bingham@worldprospect.com.

Introduction

Have you ever traveled in a country where you don't know the language? Maybe you're a little afraid of what might happen if you do. Will you get hopelessly lost? Will you not have a clue how to book a room, buy a ticket, or read a schedule? Will you order something horrible to eat because you don't know any better? And perhaps the biggest fear of all, will you make an absolute fool of yourself because you don't know any of the local customs? This is a pretty grim scenario. Almost enough to keep a would-be traveler at home. But it doesn't have to be that way!

There is a world of difference between being in a foreign country knowing nothing of the language and being in the country knowing a little of it. The first experience is confusing, frustrating and frequently misleading. (I write as one who accidently ordered two lunches for myself at the same time during my first visit to Italy, when I could not communicate beyond *yes, no, hello* and *excuse me*.)

The second experience, with just a little knowledge of the language, brims with understanding and communication, by comparison. Instead of skittering along the surface of a foreign culture, you are able to dive into it, understand some of it and participate in it. Traveling becomes a rich, heady adventure. You don't just look at museums and visit churches; you participate in the day-to-day culture of a country and its people.

Surprisingly, you don't have to devote months of time and effort to reap the benefits of a foreign language. At the start, you get huge returns for your efforts. Every little bit helps, no matter how advanced you are, but the gains are even greater at the beginning. Going from zero language knowledge to a little bit is an amazing leap in ability.

You may think you don't need to know anything about a foreign language to travel in Europe, because everyone speaks English. I hate to disillusion you, but that's not exactly true. Yes, most young people now study English, and yes, people involved in tourism will usually speak at least some English, but many, many people are uncomfortable with English or simply don't know it at all. This is particularly true off the beaten path, in areas that aren't inundated with tourists, and with middle-aged and older people. Granted, you can get by with English and gestures, but that approach can be very frustrating. Plus, with such a language handicap, you will learn and experience a lot less of the country.

It may be especially tempting not to bother learning a new language if you will be with a guided tour group. Don't be lulled into overlooking *some* language preparation! People respond so warmly to attempts to use their language. Besides, common courtesy dictates that you should at least be able to say things like "Excuse me" and "Thank you" in a way that people in your host country will understand.

Learning a foreign language really involves learning a foreign culture, too. What good does it do to know the right words and phrases if you don't know the right time to use them? This *Survival Guide*, like any other good introduction to a foreign language, includes pertinent cultural information. Knowing about culture is important for linguistic reasons, but also so you can fit in better, so you can avoid offending people, and so you can appreciate what the locals are doing. Knowing some of the culture *and* some of the language allows you to communicate more completely and have a deeper, more satisfying experience in a foreign country. And even better, the cultural information is painless to learn. As social creatures, we like to learn about how people are like and different from ourselves.

Ideally, we would all learn a foreign language and culture before traveling abroad. You may even have bought language CDs or thought about enrolling in a course with that noble purpose in mind. Realistically, though, most of us already lead full lives, and making time for language study is not a top priority. What usually happens is that time quickly runs out, and suddenly it's a mere week before departure (or maybe even the plane flight overseas) before we get serious about tackling the language of the country we are about to visit. That's the reality this *Survival Guide* is designed to meet. It provides the most important language and cultural information to people with limited time to learn it.

You will learn the basics here: travel vocabulary, super-basic grammar, everyday cultural information. All you need to add later is a small dictionary or phrase book (for extra vocabulary) and at least one sightseeing guide and you're good to go. Armed with these resources and a little training beforehand, you are sure to have a successful visit. You can be a confident, savvy foreign traveler, communicating with the locals, participating in daily life, and experiencing the culture firsthand.

Please, let me know how both your studies and your trip turn out. I would like to know what worked for you and how I can make this book better for others. You can reach me via e-mail at bingham@worldprospect.com or care of World Prospect Press, PO Box 253, Waverly, IA 50677. If you'd like, you can follow me on Facebook at Elizabeth Bingham, Author.

I wish you good luck, successful studies, and happy travels!

What about Switzerland?

This guide will prepare you to travel in Switzerland, in addition to
Germany and Austria. Switzerland is not specifically targeted in
the title or the content of the book because, sitting at the cross-
roads between Germany, Austria, Italy and France, it is more
linguistically and culturally diverse than its Germanic neighbors.
However, German is one of the official languages of Switzerland
(although it may not sound much like the German you will hear
elsewhere). In addition, northern and eastern parts of Switzerland
have close ties to Germany and Austria, and Germanic culture
and language predominate.

Disclaimer

German language and Germanic culture can vary greatly from
place to place and among different users in the same place.
Regional, generational and socioeconomic variations remain
strong to this day. While the language and culture tips offered in
this book represent common usage and practices, they do not
cover all the variation of speech and custom one may see in
Germany and Austria. Rest assured that you can communicate
with others using the material you learn from this book, even
though people may pronounce words differently, have entirely
different words for things, or have different local customs. All
German speakers can understand "standard" German, even if
that's not what they speak themselves, and you should not offend
anyone if you follow the customs discussed in these pages.

1   Greetings and Introductions

Willkommen!

Welcome to *German Survival Guide*, the down-to-earth, bare-bones introduction to German that aims to make your trip abroad as smooth and enjoyable as possible with minimal preparation. In a perfect world, all travelers would have time to take a few courses in the language of the country they are going to visit. Unfortunately, that's a reality for very few of us. Time is precious, and most language courses are long, because—let's face it—languages are complicated. That's where this *Survival Guide* comes in. It's an information-packed mini-course that concentrates on preparing you to travel in Germany and Austria in the shortest time possible. How does it accomplish this?

- It cuts out unnecessary vocabulary and grammar, focusing on what is most useful to you as a traveler.
- It relates the most important aspects of culture that you will encounter.
- It gives you lots of opportunity to practice with built-in exercises.
- It provides study tips, so you can use your preparation time most efficiently.
- It tells you what you can safely skip, if you're short on time.

This *Survival Guide* won't make you fluent in German. It's not magic. But it *will* help you communicate in the German language and culture. It will prepare you for what to expect as a traveler and how to deal with it, what to say and when to say it. As with any other skill, learning a foreign language does require some effort, and you get out of it what you put into it. That doesn't need to scare you off, though. Realistically, most travelers don't need to know that much of a foreign language to benefit from it. So, do what you can and enjoy your growing ability to communicate in German!

Absolute bare-bones German
Even if you acquire nothing else in German, do learn to say the
following phrases. You will communicate on a very basic level
and will earn good will for using some of the local language.

yes	ja	*yah*
no	nein	*nine*
please	bitte	*bit-eh*
thank you	danke	*dahnk-eh*
excuse me	Entschuldigung	*ent-shool-dig-ung*

Study tip: Practice speaking the language as much as you can.
Read aloud as you go through vocabulary lists and work on
written exercises. Every bit of practice helps. When you have
completed a lesson, go through it again, practicing how to say
things. Try to imagine yourself in the situations described and
see what you can remember how to say. Try to find someone to
practice *with*.

Study tip: What can you cut if you are pressed for time? The
exercises, grammar tips and any vocabulary sections that you
know you won't need (such as renting a car). At the very least
learn greetings, manners, and some numbers, along with simple
but very useful words like *yes*, *no* and *help*. The culture notes are
interesting and worth reading, even if you are short on time.

Study tip: If you have the time, use the exercises as a review to
test what you learned earlier. Cover up any answers you wrote
previously, and see whether you can do the exercises orally. If you
can say your answers without too much effort at home, you will
be well prepared to speak German abroad.

Importance of pronunciation: While you can let a lot of
grammar slide and still communicate perfectly well, you need a
reasonably close pronunciation of words or people won't know
what you are talking about.

Pronunciation guide

Many consonants sound the same in German as in English. Exceptions are noted in the table below. Vowels are pronounced a little differently. With all vowels, try not to move your lips and tongue as you say them—German vowels are "purer" than American ones. **Please go over the pronunciation guide below** before trying the German pronunciations written in this book, so you can become familiar with the symbols used.

The following table will help you pronounce new words in German. It's a little simplified, but is close enough to be useful. Read it across like this: "The German letter *a* is pronounced like the English sound "ah" in *father* and can be found in the words *Vater* and *Samstag*." American English pronunciation is used in the English examples.

German	Pron. Symbol	English	Example
a	ah	father	Vater, Samstag
e	e or eh	peck	der, Decke
eh or e	ay	hay	verstehe, zehn, wer
i	i	it	ich, bin
ih	ee	bee	Ihr, ihn
o	oh	oh	Boden, Woche
o	o	off	Post, voll
u	oo	cool	Stuhl, Nudeln
u	u	put	und, Mutter
ie	ee	bee	Sie, Bier
ei	y or i_e	sly, nine	nein, eins
eu	oy	boy	heute, neun
au	ow or au	ouch	auf, Haus
j	y	yak	ja, Januar
v	f	fan	von, verstehe
w	v	van	Wagen, Woche
z	ts	cats	zu, Zimmer
ß	s	sail	heißen, dreißig
sch	sh	shoot	schön, Tisch
tsch	ch	chop	Deutschland

In many varieties of German, certain letters are pronounced differently depending on whether they are in front of another vowel in the same word. (See below.) For example, the letter *d* sounds like "d" if it is in front of a vowel, as in *das* (the). If it's not followed by a vowel, though, as in *Rad* (bicycle), then *d* sounds like *t* (*Rad* sounds like *Rat*). Don't worry about this too much—it's all spelled out in the pronunciations.

German	English	Example
if not in front of a vowel		
d	t	Ra<u>d</u>
b	p	Lo<u>b</u>
g	k*	Ta<u>g</u>
r	"ah"	Mo<u>r</u>gen

* The exception to the "*g* sounds like *k* if it's not right in front of a vowel" rule is the combination *-ig*. In that situation, the *g* sounds like a front *ch* (see below), as in *windig* (windy), which is pronounced <u>vin</u>-di *ch*. Again, this is covered in the pronunciations, so you don't need to figure it out here. And if you end up going through Germany happily making all your *-ig* endings into hard *k* sounds, that's fine, too.

The German *ch*

The common letter combination of *ch* is pronounced differently depending on whether it follows a "front" vowel—i or e—or a "back" vowel—a, o, u. After an i or e, *ch* is pronounced at the top front of the mouth, behind the ridge of teeth, and sounds like a cat's hiss. Try hissing like a cat. Then say the English word "ick" but extend the end of the word, letting the air flow through behind that ridge to make a hissing sound. That's how you make the German front *ch* sound in the word *i<u>ch</u>* or *Be<u>ch</u>er*.

To make the back *ch* sound, find where you make the "ck" sound in the English word "lock." Now let air pass through that location, as in the English word loch. (To me this sounds like the gargly rasp of the dentist's suction tube.) Now say the German word *auch* ("ow-ch"). Go back and forth between the front *ich* and the back *auch* to familiarize yourself with the difference in sound and production.

Note: In the symbols for the *ch* sounds, the *ch* is raised (ᶜʰ) to show when the sound should be made at the front of the mouth (iᶜʰ), and lowered (𝒸ₕ) to show when it should be made at the back of the mouth (au𝒸ₕ).

German	Symbol	Examples
ch, after i or e	ᶜʰ, as in iᶜʰ	i<u>ch</u>, Be<u>ch</u>er
ch, after a, o, u	𝒸ₕ, as in au𝒸ₕ	au<u>ch</u>, ho<u>ch</u>

The letter *r*

The letter *r* deserves its own discussion, because it is pronounced so differently in German than in American English, and its pronunciation differs depending on whether it's in front of a vowel or not. Most of the time, *r* is not in front of a vowel and it is de-emphasized. When you need to back off the *r*, that is indicated in word pronunciations in this book by *(r)*, an *r* in parentheses, reminding you to de-emphasize the sound. Think of a British accent and how the letter *r* sounds—*mother* sounds more like "muth-ah." That's what you need to aim for in German, too. *Morgen* (morning) sounds more like "<u>moh</u>-again," said quickly, with nothing that sounds like an *r* to American ears.

English	German	Pronunciation
morning	Morgen	*mo<u>(r)</u>-gen*
October	Oktober	*ok-<u>toh</u>-be(r)*

On the other hand, if the *r* is in *front* of a vowel, especially in a stressed syllable, the *r* is often rolled at the back of the throat (like gargling) or trilled at the tip of the tongue, in Austria. When this roll is drawn out, it sounds rather like a cat purring. That's just for practice, though. Don't try to extend your roll or trill like that when speaking. In real speech, the roll is usually short, more a gravelly little rough patch than a purr, but it's definitely not a flat, broad American *r*. Even if you don't get a good roll, do your best to avoid the American *r*—it sounds really obvious and out of place in a German pronunciation. A back *ch*-sound as a replacement will get you close. To remind you to change your *r*-sound in German, the *r*'s in front of a vowel that are produced in the back of your throat are indicated in word pronunciations by an R.

English	German	Pronunciation
red	rot	*Roht*
Friday	Freitag	*fRy-tahk*

The letter *s*
if in front of a vowel, then a single *s* sounds like *z*

s	z	Sie, Samstag

if in front of *p* or *t* at the start of a syllable, then *s* sounds like *sh*

s	sh	spät, Stadt

Umlauts (simplified)
Umlauts are the two dots found over some vowels in German. *Laut* means *sound*, and *um* indicates a change or shift. Thus, an umlaut means that the sound of the vowel is changed. For example, *ö* looks like *o*, but it sounds different.

Two of the umlauted letters (*ö* and *ü*) require you to round your lips, similar to the way you do when you make the "oo" sound in *who*. For example, to pronounce an *ö*, you make the sound "ay" (as in *hay*) and round your lips around it. You can hear the sound change as your lips form a smaller opening. To make the *ü*, you make the sound "ee" and round your lips around it.

Noting "ay plus rounding" in the pronunciation for every *ö* would be too awkward, so that pronunciation is represented by the letters *er* in the pronunciation guides. (Remember to back off the *r*, softening it from the American *r*.) The other rounded letter, *ü*, is represented by *ew*, as in the English word "dew." In both these cases—*ö* and *ü*—try to remember to round your lips as you say them.

German	Pron. Symbol	English	Example
ö	er	h<u>er</u>	sch<u>ö</u>n, m<u>ö</u>chte
ü	ew	d<u>ew</u>	T<u>ü</u>r, gr<u>ü</u>n
ä[1]	eh	p<u>e</u>ck	W<u>ä</u>nde, h<u>ä</u>tte
ä[2]	ay	h<u>ay</u>	K<u>ä</u>se, R<u>ä</u>der

[1] if short (usually in front of 2 consonants)
[2] if long (not in front of 2 consonants)

Exercise 1.1
That's a lot of pronunciation rules to absorb at once. Try some exercises to get used to the way German letters represent sounds.

Which pronunciation is correct for the underlined letters in each line?

Letter(s)		Sounds like?
1. Han<u>d</u>	d	t
2. <u>d</u>er	d	t
3. <u>v</u>erstehe	v	f
4. <u>w</u>er	v	f
5. S<u>ie</u>	ee	eye
6. kl<u>ei</u>n	ee	eye
7. Bie<u>r</u>	R	(ṛ) (= "ah")
8. <u>R</u>ad	R	(ṛ)

Answers: 1) t, 2) d, 3) f, 4) v, 5) ee, 6) eye, 7) (ṛ), 8) R

Letter(s)		Sounds like?
1. Ta<u>g</u>	g	k
2. <u>g</u>ehen	g	k
3. Essi<u>g</u>	g	ch
4. Kr<u>au</u>t	ow	oy

5. h<u>eu</u>	ow	oy
6. Ra<u>d</u>	d	t
7. g<u>r</u>ün	R	(r)
8. <u>z</u>ehn	z	ts

Answers: 1) k, 2) g, 3) ch, 4) ow, 5) oy, 6) t, 7) R, 8) ts

<u>Letter(s)</u>	<u>Sounds like?</u>	
1. <u>J</u>acke	j	y
2. Kal<u>b</u>	b	p
3. <u>B</u>rot	b	p
4. f<u>ü</u>r	ew	oo
5. Br<u>ö</u>tchen	er	oh
6. H<u>u</u>t	u	oo
7. Br<u>o</u>t	er	oh
8. Spa<u>ß</u>	b	s

Answer: 1) y, 2) p, 3) b, 4) ew, 5) er, 6) oo, 7) oh, 8) s

<u>Letter(s)</u>	<u>Sounds like?</u>	
1. we<u>r</u>	R	(r)
2. <u>zwo</u>	zwoh	tsvoh
3. <u>Eu</u>ro	ew	oy
4. fr<u>ei</u>	ee	eye
5. B<u>ie</u>r	ee	eye
6. <u>J</u>unge	j	y
7. <u>weiß</u>	weeb	vice
8. J<u>ä</u>nner	ah	eh

Answers: 1) (r), 2) tsvoh, 3) oy, 4) eye, 5) ee, 6) y, 7) vice, 8) eh

Reality check: Remember, you are not in this alone! Don't worry too much if you can't seem to get the hang of how letters are pronounced. Pronunciations are written throughout this book, including in the English-German dictionary.

Greetings

A good place to start when learning a new language is with greetings. If you can say hello to people, chances are they will find you friendly and will think well of you, even if you can't say anything else in their language.

good morning	Guten Morgen!	<u>goo</u>-ten <u>moh(r)</u>-gen
good day	Guten Tag!	<u>goo</u>-ten tahk
good evening	Guten Abend!	<u>goo</u>-ten <u>ah</u>-bent
southern greeting, any time	Grüß Gott!	gRews got
Austrian greeting, any time, informal	Servus!	<u>zeh(r)</u>-voos

---

Culture note—Greetings

There are no hard-and-fast rules on when *Guten Morgen* should turn into *Guten Tag*, or when *Guten Tag* should change to *Guten Abend*. *Guten Morgen* is confined to early morning in some areas, with people saying *Guten Tag* by mid-morning. In other places, though, *Guten Morgen* takes you straight through to noon. In either case, *Guten Tag* then stretches until evening, when it will overlap with *Guten Abend* for a while. In regions as diverse as Hamburg in the north to Vienna in the southeast, some people will greet others at noontime with *Mahlzeit!*, which means "Have a good meal!"

Distinctions in greeting may have more to do with frame of mind (or amount of daylight) than actual time. For some people, *Guten Abend* is what they use after supper. When people have not been up long, they say *Guten Morgen*; when they're done working for the day, they say *Guten Abend*; and everything in between is *Guten Tag*. It's a theory, anyway. Things are much simpler in Austria, where you can confidently greet with *Grüß Gott!* regardless of the time.

Study tip: Do the exercises if you have time to. If you don't have time, skip them. They help, but you can get by with oral practice.

Exercise 1.2

Which greeting is most appropriate for each situation?

1. 3 p.m. in Berlin

2. Noon in Vienna

3. 8 a.m. in Hamburg

4. 9 p.m. in Frankfurt

5. 6 p.m. in Salzburg

Answers: 1) Guten Tag, 2) Grüß Gott/Servus, 3) Guten Morgen, 4) Guten Abend, 5) Grüß Gott/Servus

---

Culture note—Formality

German culture is more formal than American culture. For instance, Germans and Austrians tend to be reserved with people they don't know well. This reserve or "stiffness" is not unfriendliness, but rather the result of different cultural rules. Germans, by and large, do not rush into new relationships and informality the way Americans do. Rest assured, however, that once friendships are established, Germans and Austrians are every bit as warm and demonstrative as you might wish. And, for better or worse, you may discover that forging new relationships goes into fast forward if you end up sharing a table with locals in a beer hall or wine garden.

Culture note—Titles

Herr, Frau, Fräulein. One sign of greater formality in Germany and Austria is the use of titles rather than given names. Neighbors who have known each other for decades and talk over the fence daily may still address each other as "Herr Braun" and "Frau Meier." All adult women are addressed as *Frau*, regardless of their marital status. As a German friend told me, "Nobody cares anymore whether you're married or not." *Fräulein* is used only for young, unmarried girls. When in doubt about which title to use for a woman or older teenager, use *Frau*.

Introductions

One of the joys of travel is meeting new people. Here are three common forms of introduction. Learn how to introduce yourself and ask others their names.

Literally, How are you called?	Wie heißen Sie?	*vee <u>hy</u>-sen zee?*
I am called ___.	Ich heiße ___.	*i^{ch} <u>hy</u>-seh ___*
What is your name?	Wie ist Ihr Name?	*vee ist ee(r) <u>nah</u>-meh?*
My name is ___.	Mein Name ist ___.	*mine <u>nah</u>-meh ist ___*
Who are you?	Wer sind Sie?	*vay(r) zint zee?*
I am ___.	Ich bin ___.	*i^{ch} bin ___*
And you?	Und Sie?	*unt zee?*

💣 Warning: Watch out for the German word *wer*. It looks like *where*, but it means *who*. *Wer sind Sie?* is asking *who* you are, not *where* you are. The German word for *where* is *wo*.

Study tip: You may "mix and match" question and answer forms in introductions. For example, if someone asks the question, "Wie heißen Sie?", it is perfectly appropriate to answer, "Mein Name ist _____." If you find the variations confusing, a good strategy is to recognize the different ways people can ask you your name, but always respond with the form you feel most comfortable with.

Exercise 1.3
Practice introducing yourself and asking other people their name. Practice all three forms.

1. What are three ways you can you introduce yourself?
2. What are three ways you can ask someone their name?

Answers: 1) Ich heiße/Ich bin/Mein Name ist ___. 2) Wie heißen Sie?/Wer sind Sie?/Wie ist Ihr Name?

Culture note—The gracious guest

Germans and Austrians do not often invite new acquaintances into their homes. It's a bit of an honor if you receive such an invitation. You should arrive on time, that is, not early and not more than five minutes late. (Germans tend to be very punctual.) You might also bring a small gift for your hosts, such as flowers, a small box of nice chocolates, or something from your own country. If you bring flowers, have the florist help you choose something appropriate, and remove the wrapping before giving them to your hosts. In some homes, you may be asked to remove your shoes upon entering. Your hosts may offer you house slippers to wear during your stay. While customs for adults vary, children are usually expected to remove their shoes at the door.

Culture note—Language formality

The German language, like many others, preserves a distinction in formality that the English language has long since dropped. There is a formal way to address people, the *Sie* ("zee") form, as well as an informal way, the *du* ("due") form. German speakers usually address people they don't know well or whom they know in formal contexts (such as white-collar co-workers) with the formal *Sie* form.

Addressing someone with the wrong level of formality can cause offense, particularly if you are too informal. Because travelers interact primarily if not exclusively with strangers, this guide focuses on the *Sie* form.

Do note, however, that family members use the *du* form with each other. Thus, if you visit German relatives, they will probably use the *du* form with you, even though you may never have met them before. When they realize that you only know the *Sie* form, they should not be offended if you do not reciprocate with the same informality they use. If you think you will need the informal form, look at the a short introduction of the *du* form near the end of this book. (See p. 144.)

Culture note—Introductions

About that German formality. . . . If you are meeting non-relatives, you should generally introduce yourself by using your last name with or without a title: "Ich bin Frau Schneider." "Ich heiße Bachmann," or you can use your first and last names: "Elizabeth Bingham," "Guten Tag. Reinhard Schmidt." An introduction is usually accompanied by a firm handshake and often a decisive nod. Traditionally, you will just shake (and nod) once. However, some people will use a more "American" greeting if they realize you are from the United States. Approach an introduction expecting to greet "German style," but let the other person take the lead. If the other person starts shaking your hand more than once, go along with it.

Relatives and young people will introduce themselves with their first names but may still shake hands. Even children have learned to greet others by shaking their hands. (American children are encouraged to participate in this polite ritual. It demonstrates good manners.) You won't mortally offend anyone if you forget all this handshaking stuff or you tell everyone your first name, but knowing the customs can make introductions a little smoother.

A word about grammar

Knowing a little bit of grammar can make using a language easier, because you can see some of the language's underlying system, the order, the rules for how things work. This book presents small "bites" of grammar throughout. If you find them interesting or useful, great! Follow the rules and make your German more grammatically accurate. If you find grammar to be boring or confusing, skip the grammar sections. Grammaticality is the frosting on the foreign language cake. It makes things "look" nice, "taste" a little sweeter, but the main component of communication (the "cake," so to speak) is vocabulary. Ideally you will learn vocabulary and grammar hand in hand, but if you have limited time and have to choose between grammar and vocabulary, definitely concentrate on vocabulary. You will get a lot more bang for your buck there.

Grammar—Present tense verb endings

Subject	Verb Ending	Example
ich (I)	-e	ich spreche
Sie (you)	-en	Sie sprechen

One of the most useful aspects of grammar to learn is how to handle verbs. If your verb forms are correct, your German will be easier to understand.

Verbs are usually listed in language books and dictionaries in the *infinitive* form. The infinitive form is the basic form of the verb, the form it is in before we start changing it to show who or what is doing the action (which is called *inflecting* the verb). In English, the infinitive form of a verb uses the word *to* followed by the verb, for example, *to be*. That is why translations of German verbs are usually listed after *to*, to indicate that the verbs are in their basic, unchanged, infinitive state.

German infinitive	English translation
sprechen	to speak
heißen	to be called
kommen	to come
haben	to have

When we *inflect* the verb, we change it to show who or what is doing the action. The English verb forms *is*, *am* and *are* are all inflected forms of the verb *to be*. In English (or whatever your native language is) you automatically know how to inflect the verb.

Even though the inflection is automatic, it still follows rules of the language that you internalized at a very early age and don't even have to think about. When we learn a foreign language, most of us have to think about the rules, at least until we get enough experience that they become automatic, too. Here are the rules for inflecting almost all German verbs (summarized in the table at the top of this section).

The verb in infinitive form consists of two parts, the stem and an -en (or -n) ending. For example, here are some verbs that you will see in this chapter, with a hyphen added to separate the stem from the ending: *heiß-en* (to be called), *komm-en* (to come), *versteh-en* (to understand), *wiederhol-en* (to repeat), *sprech-en* (to speak).

With almost all verbs, you start with the stem of the verb, for example *sprech-*, and add to it to show who the verb refers to. If you want to talk about yourself, you will use the word *ich* (I) and will add the ending *-e* to the verb stem: *ich spreche* (I speak). If you are talking directly to someone (usually using a question or command), use the word *Sie* (you) and add the ending *-en* to the verb stem: *Sie sprechen* (you speak), or, more likely, *Sprechen Sie. . .?* (Do you speak. . .?). Notice that the *Sie*-form of the verb (*Sie sprechen*) is the same as the infinitive form (*sprechen*). That means you don't have to learn anything new for it; just use the infinitive form. The only thing you really need to remember, then, is that the *ich*-form of the verb ends just in *-e*, not *-en*.

One big exception to the verb inflection rules is the verb *to be*, which is highly irregular in all western European languages, including English. In German, the infinitive form of *to be* is *sein*, but the inflected forms are *ich bin* and *Sie sind*. You have to memorize these forms.

Study tip: If your goal is to learn more German in the future, to be as proficient as possible, you should be as accurate as you can. Read and use the grammar tips, pay attention to your verb endings, learn the gender of nouns (we'll get to this on p. 40). If your main goal is to communicate the best you can with the least commitment of time, then don't worry about grammar and accuracy; focus on vocabulary.

Exercise 1.4
Practice putting these verbs into the correct form (*ich* or *Sie*).

1. I speak (*sprechen*)

2. you speak

3. I hear (*hören*)

4. you hear

5. I understand (*verstehen*)

6. you understand

7. I'm coming (*kommen*)

8. you come

9. I have (*haben*)

10. you have

Answers: 1) ich spreche, 2) Sie sprechen, 3) ich höre, 4) Sie hören, 5) ich verstehe, 6) Sie verstehen, 7) ich komme, 8) Sie kommen, 9) ich habe, 10) Sie haben

---

Culture note—Group introductions

Introductions can become quite a production in Germany and Austria. If you are being introduced to several people at once, be prepared to shake everyone's hand and to exchange names with everyone. I was once the amused onlooker to two parties (all acquaintances of mine) who were introducing themselves to each other, the Ganglmair family (of three adults) and the Holzer family (of two adults). The introductions went something like this:

> "Ganglmair." "Holzer." (Handshake.)
> "Holzer." "Ganglmair." (Handshake.)
> "Holzer." "Ganglmair." (Handshake.)
> "Ganglmair." "Holzer." (Handshake.)
> "Ganglmair." "Holzer." (Handshake.)
> "Holzer." "Ganglmair." (Handshake.)

All three Ganglmairs had to introduce themselves to both Holzers and vice versa. This is certainly overkill by American standards, but when in Rome (or Vienna). . . . Again, it's best to follow whatever everyone else is doing.

Grammar—Forming questions

There are several ways to form questions in German, just as there are in English. In German, though, you usually have to shift the words around a bit to make the question clear and accurate. Actually, you need to change the word order for most English questions, too, but it's so automatic that you probably don't even notice the shift.

Consider this English sentence and some corresponding questions:

> The hat costs 30 euros.
>
> 1. <u>Does</u> the hat cost 30 euros?
>
> 2. <u>How much does</u> the hat cost?

In both questions, you change the word order, starting the question with something other than "the hat."

In German, questions follow much the same pattern. Starting with the "answer" of *Der Hut kostet 30 Euro*, let's see what some logical questions would be.

First, you can switch the subject (*der Hut*) and the verb (*kostet*) to form a question.

1. Kostet	der Hut	30 Euro?
(verb)	(subject)	(rest of sentence)

Or you can start the question with a question word, then the verb.

2. Wieviel	kostet	der Hut?
(Q-word)	(verb)	(subject)

Another way to ask questions is perhaps less polished but works in either language—simply use the statement form, but make your voice rise questioningly at the end: "The hat costs 30 euros?" or *"Der Hut kostet 30 Euro?"* Most of the time, this simpler form will work just fine.

Exercise 1.5
Practice changing these sentences into logical questions.

1. Sie sprechen Englisch.
2. Sie haben Zimmer frei.
3. Ich habe genug Geld.
4. Ich bin zu spät.
5. Der Bus fährt zum Schloß.
6. Der Bahnhof ist in der Nähe.

Answers: 1) Sprechen Sie English? 2) Haben Sie Zimmer frei? 3) Habe ich genug Geld? 4) Bin ich zu spät? 5) Fährt der Bus zum Schloß?/Wohin fährt der Bus? 6) Ist der Bahnhof in der Nähe?/Wo ist der Bahnhof?

Origins
It seems that people always want to know where travelers are from. Be prepared to recognize these questions and know how to answer them.

where from?	woher?	*voh-hay(r)?*
Where do you come from?	Woher kommen Sie?	*voh-hay(r) kom-en zee?*
I come from ___.	Ich komme aus ___.	*i^{ch} kom-eh ows ___*
Where are you from?	Woher sind Sie?	*voh-hay(r) zint zee?*
I am from ___.	Ich bin aus ___.	*i^{ch} bin ows ___*
And you?	Und Sie?	*unt zee?*

Again, you can mix and match question and answer forms.

Some country names
Germany	Deutschland	*doych-lahnt*
Austria	Österreich	*er-steh(r)-Ry^{ch}*
Switzerland	die Schweiz	*dee shvyts*
Italy	Italien	*ee-tahl-yen*
France	Frankreich	*fRahnk-Ry^{ch}*
Spain	Spanien	*shpahn-yen*

England	England	*eng-lahnt*
the United States	Amerika	*ah-may-Ree-kah*
	die Vereinigten Staaten	*dee feh(r)-eye-nik-ten shtah-ten*
Canada	Kanada	*kah-nah-dah*
Australia	Australien	*ow-stRahl-yen*

Directional phrases

north of	nördlich von	*nerd-li^ch fon*
south of	südlich von	*zewd-li^ch fon*
east of	östlich von	*erst-li^ch fon*
west of	westlich von	*vest-li^ch fon*

Culture note—Origins

In Germany and Austria, *Amerika* means the United States. You can refer to the United States as *die USA* or *die Vereinigten Staaten*, but German/Austrian custom is just to call it *Amerika*.

Unless you live in a large and well-known city (New York, Chicago, Miami, Los Angeles, Dallas) or in a well-known state (New York, Florida, Texas, California), most people won't recognize the place name or know where it is. To give them an idea, tell where your home is in relation to a place people might know. For example, an exchange with me might run like this:

> "Woher kommen Sie, Frau Bingham?"
> "Ich komme aus Amerika."
> "Und wo wohnen Sie in Amerika?"
> ("And where do you live in America?")
> "In Iowa, westlich von Chicago."

If they already know I'm American, I could just say, "Ich komme aus Iowa, westlich von Chicago." This won't help all the time, but it's a start. Most people will recognize the name "Chicago," even if they can't all place it on a map.

Exercise 1.6
Practice the different ways of asking and telling about origin.

1. Ask someone where he or she is from.
2. Tell where you are from.

Answers: 1) Woher sind Sie? Woher kommen Sie? 2) Ich bin aus ___. Ich komme aus ___.

Culture note—North-South differences

It's always dangerous to generalize about people according to geography, but usually there's at least a grain of truth to geograph-ical stereotypes. Here are some commonly held beliefs about how people in northern Germany differ from those in southern Germany and Austria.

The stereotypical northerner is earnest, industrious, and very concerned about productivity, punctuality and protocol. North-erners also know how to have fun, of course, and typically have a wonderful sense of humor, but somehow life in the north seems more serious and high-pressured than in the south.

The stereotypical southerner (living in Austria or Bavaria, for the most part) can seem laid-back compared to a northern counter-part. Work gets done—typically with great efficiency—but the pace of life seems slower, with more time to stop and taste the beer (or wine). Bavaria and Austria both have strong tourist industries that reinforce the lighthearted, happy images of those regions.

To many people, northern Germany represents the economic miracle of recovery after the war, success built on hard work and discipline, while Bavaria stands for Oktoberfest and fantastic castles, and Austria represents Mozart, mountains and *The Sound of Music.*

These thumbnail impressions don't do justice to the complexity of Germany and Austria, of course, but as superficial descriptions, they give a sense of how the regions "feel" to many tourists.

Leave-taking

Just as you will want to say hello to people, you'll want to say goodbye. Feel free to learn one form well and stick with it.

goodbye	(Auf) Wiedersehen!	*(owf)* <u>*vee*</u>*-deh(r)-zayn*
	(Auf) Wiederschauen!	*(owf)* <u>*vee*</u>*-deh(r)-shau-en*
'bye (Germany)	Tschüs!	*chews*
'bye (Austria)	Servus!	<u>*zeh(r)*</u>*-voos*

Gute Nacht (<u>*goo*</u>*-teh nah*_{*ch*}*t*) is what you say upon going to bed. Even if you leave a party late in the night, you would say *Auf Wiedersehen* (or its equivalent).

Culture note—Regional vocabulary

Each region and most cities within a region will have at least some words, pronunciations, or other language uses all their own. One of the larger language differences within the German-speaking world is the different vocabulary used in most of Germany versus what is often used in Austria. (Bavaria is linguistically and culturally linked to Austria. You will hear some "Austrian" words also being used in parts of Bavaria.) Here is a short list, highlighting some differences among common words.

English	German	Austrian
roll	Brötchen	Semmel
corn	Mais	Kukuruz
tomato	Tomate	Paradeiser
potato	Kartoffel	Erdapfel
grape	Traube	Weintraube
apricot	Aprikose	Marille
plum	Pflaume	Zwetschge
dumpling	Kloß	Knödel
turkey	Truthahn	Puter
this year	dieses Jahr	heuer
January	Januar	Jänner
mosquito	Mücke	Gelse

Useful Expressions

yes	ja	*yah*
no	nein	*nine*
and	und	*unt*
or	oder	*oh-deh(r)*
not	nicht	*ni^{ch}t*
I don't understand.	Ich verstehe nicht.	*i^{ch} feh(r)-shtay-eh ni^{ch}t*
Please repeat.	Wiederholen Sie, bitte.	*vee-deh(r)-hohl-en zee, bit-eh*
Speak ___.	Sprechen Sie ___.	*shpRe^{ch}-en zee ___*
slowly	langsam	*lahng-zahm*
more loudly	lauter	*lowt-eh(r)*
Just a moment.	Moment.	*moh-ment*

Exercise 1.7

Write what you would say in each of these situations.

1. Someone is speaking too quickly.

2. You would like something repeated.

3. Someone is speaking too softly.

4. You don't understand.

Answers: 1) Sprechen Sie langsam, bitte. 2) Wiederholen Sie, bitte. 3) Sprechen Sie lauter, bitte. 4) Ich verstehe nicht.

Culture note—Servus!

Servus is the Austrian version of *ciao* or *aloha*—it can be used for coming or going, for hello or goodbye. It's less formal than *Grüß Gott!* for greeting or *Auf Wiedersehen/Auf Wiederschauen!* for parting, very common among friends and family members. Other ways to say goodbye in Austria include *Papa!* (with a sound between a /b/ and a /p/) and *Pfiati!*, if you really want to get into the local practice.

2   Lodging

Numbers (0-10)

Numbers are among the most useful vocabulary items you will learn in a foreign language. Learning all the numbers at once can be an overwhelming task, so this book breaks numbers up into five different lessons. Start at the beginning and learn to count from zero to ten.

0	null	*nul*
1	eins	*ines*
2	zwei/zwo	*tsvy/tsvoh*
3	drei	*dRy*
4	vier	*fee(r)*
5	fünf	*fewnf*
6	sechs	*ze^{ch}s*
7	sieben	<u>*zee*</u>*-ben*
8	acht	*ah$_{ch}$t*
9	neun	*noyn*
10	zehn	*tsayn*

Culture note—Counting on fingers

When Germans and Austrians count on their fingers, they start with their thumbs. Thus, a count of *one* is indicated by sticking one thumb out. *Two* is the thumb and forefinger, etc. *Six* is all five fingers on one hand and the thumb on the other hand.

It's useful to know this before ordering something at a bar or bakery or anywhere else you might indicate number by holding up fingers. For example, you could accidentally double your order if you hold your index finger up, American style, to order one beer. When the waiter sees that you have the index finger up, he might well assume that the thumb is out, too, and bring you two beers.

Exercise 2.1

After practicing the numbers to yourself, translate the following into German.

zero	three
six	nine
one	four
seven	ten
two	five
eight	

Culture note—Handwritten numbers

German numbers can be very confusing when written by hand. *Ones* have a swoop leading up to them, so they often look like *sevens* to American eyes. German speakers don't confuse them with *sevens*, though, because *sevens* have little bars crossing their stems. You will encounter handwritten numbers on bills, on some price tags, and on restaurant specials that are listed on blackboards.

Exercise 2.2

Practice some simple math.

1. vier plus drei =

2. fünf minus zwei =

3. sechs plus vier =

4. neun plus null =

5. acht minus eins minus sieben =

6. sechs minus vier =

7. eins plus drei =

8. vier plus vier =

9. null plus eins =

10. sieben minus zwei =

11. drei plus eins plus zwei =

Answers: 1) sieben, 2) drei, 3) zehn, 4) neun, 5) null, 6) zwei, 7) vier, 8) acht, 9) eins, 10) fünf, 11) sechs

---

Culture note—Hotel ratings

Many hotels are rated according to stars. One star indicates a "tourist" class hotel, pretty basic. Two stars indicate a "standard" hotel. Three stars are for "comfort" hotels. Four stars indicate a first-class hotel, and five stars represent a luxury hotel. A three-star hotel will have most of the comforts of home—private bath, TV, telephone, hair dryer, soap, shampoo and lotions, maybe a refrigerator. Frankly, I can't tell what the additional star of a four-star hotel buys you, other than a more expensive breakfast and a more crisply professional staff.

Read the hotel description online if you want to know what amenities come with your room. For most of us, two- or three-star comfort is fine. The fewer the stars, the more informal your accommodations are likely to be. Also, the more likely that you will need to supply your own soap, shampoo, and, at true budget hotels, maybe even towel. Smaller hotels and pensions might not have any star rating at all, but that doesn't mean they can't be wonderful choices, especially if they are easier on the budget.

Travel tip: Many hotels offer special rates if you stay more than a night or two. For example, if you stay four nights, you might get the fifth for free, or something like that.

Consider using a hotel for a longer stay as a base and making day trips to see the sights. This can be particularly economical if your hotel is in a rural area with lower rates, but within easy driving distance (or a convenient train or bus ride) of a number of interesting sights.

Grammar—Gender (definite articles, nominative case)

der	*the* — masculine
die	*the* — feminine
das	*the* — neuter
die	*the* — plural

In German, all nouns have a "gender." Every noun is either masculine, feminine, or neuter. This is an example of *grammatical gender*, where gender has everything to do with grammar and very little to do with natural or biological sex. For example, in German, a table is masculine, a lamp is feminine, and a window is neuter. Usually there is no clear connection between the gender of a noun and the real world. Nouns about people often have the same grammatical gender and natural gender, but they may also differ. (A man is masculine, a woman is feminine, but a girl is neuter.)

The gender of a noun affects certain words that are related to the noun, such as the word *the*. As you may know, *the* is a *definite article*, called so because it usually refers to some definite noun—*the* table, *the* book, *the* jacket. The definite article changes in German according to the gender of the noun. If a noun is masculine, *the* must also be masculine: *der* (pronounced like "dare"). For feminine nouns, *the* is expressed as *die* (pronounced "dee"), and for neuter nouns it is expressed as *das* ("dahs"). All plural nouns use the definite article *die*.

Unfortunately, the gender of nouns must usually be memorized along with the noun itself. That's why vocabulary listings in course books and dictionaries include an indication of the noun's gender: *der* or *m* for masculine, *die* or *f* for feminine, and *das* or *n* for neuter. The bad news is that grammatical gender is hard to keep straight, even for advanced students of German. The good news is that using the wrong gender with a noun will hardly ever keep people from understanding you. For the record, it's pretty easy to spot nouns in German, at least in written form. All nouns start with a capital letter, except most pronouns, such as *ich*, which are only capitalized when they start a sentence.

Culture note—Doors

In general, Germans and Austrians are much more careful about closing doors in their homes and other buildings than Americans are. This custom continues from the days before central heating, when rooms were shut off to reduce drafts and conserve heat. While energy conservation may be part of the reason for today's practice of shutting doors, people may also shut doors for an increased sense of privacy.

I've read that the compartmentalization of German homes and work places mirrors the "compartmentalization" of many German minds—home strictly separate from work, the formal separate from the informal, a fondness for fences and walls and other dividers, physical and mental. How much that observation still applies is open to discussion, but certainly less for the younger generation than older ones. Like younger Germans, modern homes are also more "open," usually with an open floor plan and fewer doors.

One door that is always shut (or barely ajar) in most homes is the bathroom door, whether the room is occupied or not.

Concrete Vocabulary

Practice identifying things around you. You can certainly get by without this vocabulary, but it's easy to practice at home, and it's quite possible that you might use some of these words at a hotel or restaurant or on a train.

What is that?	Was ist das?	*vahs ist dahs?*
That is ___.	Das ist ___.	*dahs ist ___*
room	das Zimmer	*dahs <u>tsim</u>-eh(r)*
thing	das Ding	*dahs ding*
floor	der Boden	*day(r) <u>boh</u>-den*
chair	der Stuhl	*day(r) shtool*
table	der Tisch	*day(r) tish*
wastebasket	der Papierkorb	*day(r) pah-<u>pee(r)</u>-ko(r)p*
ballpoint pen	der Kuli	*day(r) <u>koo</u>-lee*

trash can	der Abfalleimer	*day(r) ahp-fahl-ime-eh(r)*
wall	die Wand	*dee vahnt*
door	die Tür	*dee tew(r)*
ceiling	die Decke	*dee dek-eh*
light fixture/lamp	die Lampe	*dee lahm-peh*
window	das Fenster	*dahs fen-steh(r)*
light	das Licht	*dahs li^{ch}t*
book	das Buch	*dahs boo_{ch}*
paper	das Papier	*dahs pah-pee(r)*

Culture note—Calendar weeks

German calendars show the week starting on Monday, not Sunday. The entire weekend is at the end of the week. If you think about it, that makes sense, since Sunday is often considered the seventh day. Still, the difference can cause confusion, so don't assume that European calendars are set up the same as American ones. Take a good look when you refer to one.

Days of the Week

Monday	Montag	*mohn-tahk*
Tuesday	Dienstag	*deens-tahk*
Wednesday	Mittwoch	*mit-vo_{ch}*
Thursday	Donnerstag	*don-eh(r)s-tahk*
Friday	Freitag	*fRy-tahk*
Saturday	Samstag or	*zahms-tahk*
	Sonnabend	*zon-ah-bent*
Sunday	Sonntag	*zon-tahk*
the weekend	das Wochenende	*dahs vo_{ch}-en-end-eh*
today	heute	*hoy-teh*
tomorrow	morgen	*mo(r)-gen*
yesterday	gestern	*ges-teh(r)n*
when?	wann?	*vahn?*
What is today?	Was ist heute?	*vahs ist hoy-teh?*
Today is ___.	Heute ist ___.	*hoy-teh ist ___*
When is ___?	Wann ist ___?	*vahn ist ___?*

early morning	der Morgen	*day(r) mo(r)-gen*
mid- and late morning	der Vormittag	*day(r) foh(r)-mit-tahk*
afternoon	der Nachmittag	*day(r) nah_{ch}-mit-tahk*
evening	der Abend	*day(r) ah-bent*
night	die Nacht	*dee nah_{cht}*
Tuesday evening	Dienstagabend	*deens-tahk-ah-bent*
Sunday morning	Sonntagvormittag	*zon-tahk-foh(r)-mit-tahk*
Friday afternoon	Freitagnachmittag	*fRy-tahk-nah_{ch}-mit-tahk*

Exercise 2.3

Match the day of the week with the correct description. Try to figure out the unfamiliar words, knowing they have something to do with days of the week. (Or peek in the dictionary at the back of this book.)

1. _____ Donnerstag, ?? , Samstag   A. Mittwoch

2. _____ beginnt das Wochenende   B. Sonntag

3. _____ Mitte von der Woche   C. Freitag

4. _____ endet das Wochenende   D. Montag

5. _____ beginnt die Woche   E. Samstag

Answers: 1) C, 2) E, 3) A, 4) B, 5) D

Culture note—Written dates

Dates in German are written from the smallest to the largest unit, that is, day-month-year. Christmas Day would be written as 25. Dezember or, using all numerals, as 25.12. It's especially important to remember the correct order when the date happens to be 12 or smaller. While Americans might figure out that 19.7. on a schedule indicates July 19 (as there is no 19th month), we might easily forget and read 8.7. as Aug. 7, rather than July 8.

Months and Seasons

January	Januar	*yah-noo-ah(r)*
February	Februar	*feb-Roo-ah(r)*
March	März	*meh(r)ts*
April	April	*ah-pRil*
May	Mai	*my*
June	Juni	*yoo-nee*
July	Juli	*yoo-lee*
August	August	*ow-gust*
September	September	*zep-tem-beh(r)*
October	Oktober	*ok-toh-beh(r)*
November	November	*noh-vem-beh(r)*
December	Dezember	*deh-tsem-beh(r)*
spring	der Frühling	*day(r) fRoo-ling*
summer	der Sommer	*day(r) zom-eh(r)*
fall	der Herbst	*day(r) heh(r)pst*
winter	der Winter	*day(r) vin-teh(r)*
in month/season	im _____	*im___*

Exercise 2.4

Answer the following questions. Try to come up with both the correct month and season.

1. Wann ist Weihnachten (Christmastime)?

2. Wann ist Muttertag (Mother's Day)?

3. Wann ist Vatertag (Father's Day, in the U.S.)?

4. Wann ist Valentinstag?

5. Wann ist Halloween?

6. Wann ist "Thanksgiving"?

7. Wann haben Sie Geburtstag (birthday)?

Answers: 1) (Weihnachten ist) im Dezember/im Winter. 2) (Muttertag ist) im Mai/im Frühling. 3) (Vatertag ist) im Juni/im Sommer. 4) (Valentinstag ist) im Februar/im Winter. 5) (Halloween ist) im Oktober/im Herbst. 6) ("Thanksgiving" ist) im November/im Hebst. 7) (Ich habe) im your birthday month (Geburtstag).

Units of Time

how long?	wie lange?	*vee lahng-eh?*
how many?	wie viele?	*vee fee-leh?*
year	das Jahr-e	*dahs yah(r)/+eh*
month	der Monat-e	*day(r) moh-naht/+eh*
week	die Woche-n	*dee voch-eh/+n*
day	der Tag-e	*day(r) tahk/+eh*
hour	die Stunde-n	*dee shtun-deh/+n*
minute	die Minute-n	*dee mi-noo-teh/+n*
second	die Sekunde-n	*dee zeh-kun-deh/+n*

Grammar—Plural forms

You probably noticed that many of the words listed above have hyphens and letters added at the end of them. That is a traditional way of indicating what the plural form of a word is. The plural form of *Tag* (day), for example, is *Tage*. Thus, if someone asks, *Wie viele Tage sind Sie in München?* (How many days are you [going to be] in Munich?), you might answer, *drei Tage* (three days).

Unfortunately, there are many different ways of indicating plural. (See the German-English dictionary in the back for plural forms of words used in this book.) If you find plurals too confusing, just ignore them. Anyone would understand *drei Tag* just as well as you would understand *three day*. Plural forms are a nice touch of accuracy, but they add very little to communication.

Exercise 2.5

Answer the following questions about units of time. Just use numerals for numbers you haven't learned yet.

1. Wie viele Monate hat (has) ein Jahr?

2. Wie viele Wochen hat ein Jahr?

3. Wie viele Tage hat ein Jahr?

4. Wie viele Tage hat eine Woche?

5. Wie viele Stunden hat ein Tag?

6. Wie viele Minuten hat eine Stunde?

7. Wie viele Sekunden hat eine Minute?

Answers: 1) Ein Jahr hat 12 Monate. 2) Ein Jahr hat 52 Wochen. 3) Ein Jahr hat 365 Tage. 4) Eine Woche hat sieben Tage. 5) Ein Tag hat 24 Stunden. 6) Eine Stunde hat 60 Minuten. 7) Eine Minute hat 60 Sekunden.

Culture note—How not to look like a tourist

It's unlikely that you will blend so well into German society that no one will identify you as a foreigner, but you can minimize the fact that you are a tourist.

Why does it matter? For one thing, people appreciate it when visitors care enough to learn about their customs and try to fit in. You might get a warmer reception from locals that way.

For another reason, obvious tourists are vulnerable to petty crime in urban areas. The more American you look, the more some people will think you are "easy pickings." (Not that picked pockets are common in Germany or Austria, but theft does happen.)

A third reason to care is that U.S. foreign policy sometimes leads to anti-American sentiment abroad (mostly against the government, not individuals). No one is likely to say or do anything to you, but why draw attention to yourself?

If you follow these easy guidelines, you will stand out much less as an American tourist in Europe:

—don't wear white tennis shoes

—don't wear a ball cap

—don't wear white athletic socks with shorts

—don't wear short shorts, if you are a woman

—don't wear a fanny pack (backpacks are more common)

—don't talk too loudly

—don't hang a camera around your neck

—*do* attempt to use German

Culture note—Keyed electricity

If you are not able to turn on the lights in your hotel room, you probably need to insert your room key (metal key or plastic room card) into a slot by the door.

Culture note—Television

Most non-budget hotel rooms now include television, and offerings usually cover the cable or satellite spectrum. In addition to an English-speaking channel or two, there will be plenty of German-speaking ones, many showing seemingly nothing other than American series dubbed in German. You should find plenty of familiar fare (if that's what you are looking for), even if you are not able to understand all the dialogue. With the variety of offerings, be careful about letting children flip through the channels unsupervised. They could easily stumble on some pretty raunchy programs.

Culture note—Zimmer frei?

In Germany and Austria, you might choose to stay in a *Hotel*, a *Gasthaus* or *Gasthof* (inn), or a *Pension* (a guesthouse, generally more basic than a hotel). These choices will usually include breakfast, although higher prices and more stars seem to make an included breakfast *less* likely.

Another rooming option, usually budget-friendly, is to rent a room in a private home. You will see signs in windows of houses announcing *Zimmer frei* (rooms available). Go to the door and inquire. You may certainly ask to see a room before deciding whether you want it (*Könnte ich bitte das Zimmer sehen?*), and you will, of course, want to ask the price and whether it includes breakfast. In my experience, private home owners go out of their way to make a visitor's stay as warm and comfortable as possible, especially in smaller towns. One of the drawbacks of rooms in private homes is that you usually have to stumble on them in person—most are not listed on Web sites.

Grammar—definite/indefinite articles (nominative case)

	Masculine	**Feminine**	**Neuter**	**Plural**
the	der	die	das	die
	der Tag	die Lampe	das Ding	die Autos
a	ein	eine	ein	
	ein Tag	eine Lampe	ein Ding	Autos

You read earlier what a *definite article* is: some form of *the*, used to refer to a specific (or *definite*) noun, for example, *die* Lampe (*the* lamp). A different kind of article is the *indefinite article*, some form of *a* or *an*. We use an indefinite article when we aren't referring to a specific noun, but any noun of a certain type, for example, *a* lamp, instead of *the* lamp. Consider the difference in the following suggestions:

"Let's see a movie tonight." "Let's see the movie tonight."

Do you see the difference? The first sentence suggests seeing *a* movie (any would do), while the second sentence suggests seeing a particular movie, *the* movie.

Like English, German uses different words for *a* and *the*. As we already know, *the* is based on some form of *der*, *die* or *das*, depending on the gender and number of the noun (whether it's singular or plural). The options for *a* are a little more limited. For most of what we will be doing, the indefinite article (*a*) for masculine and neuter nouns will be *ein* and the indefinite article for feminine nouns will be *eine*. There is no plural form of *a*.

Reality check: No one will throw you out of the country if you mess up your articles. If you like to be as accurate as possible, by all means work on using definite and indefinite articles appropriately. If you can't keep them straight, or if you are really short on time, don't worry about them.

Concrete vocabulary review

Practice asking and answering questions using the concrete
vocabulary from p. 41. Try to decide whether you would use *the*
or *a* if you were speaking English, and then use the German
version of that. Can you identify things in the room you are in?

What's that?	Was ist das?
That's the _____.	Das ist der/die/das _____.
That's a _____.	Das ist ein/eine _____.

Culture note—Light switches

Hotels and guesthouses and some homes have traditionally used
timed lights in the hallways. Push the light switch—often visible
as a glowing button in the dark—and continue to or from your
room. The light will turn off automatically. Many hotels have
replaced the timed lights in hallways with motion-detecting lights,
which makes navigating the hallway easier.

Culture note—Feather beds

Most beds in homes and hotels will not feature the typical sheet/
blanket/bedspread set found in American homes and hotels.
Germans and Austrians usually combine the top sheet and
blanket into a feather bed, a puffy, feather-filled comforter that is
encased in the "sheet," a duvet. The feather bed is generally
folded in half and laid on the bed to "make" the bed—much
easier than making an American-style bed. There is usually no
separate bedspread.

My daughter absolutely loves the puffy feather beds and feather
pillows in Germany and Austria. My husband, allergic to feathers,
is less enthusiastic. If feathers are a problem for you, you might
tell your hotel clerk, *Ich bin allergisch gegen Federn. Könnte ich bitte eine
Decke ohne Federn haben?* (I'm allergic to feathers. Could I please
have a blanket without feathers?)

Manners

It always pays to be polite when you are traveling in a foreign country. Learning how to say *please*, *thank you* and *excuse me* should be a top priority.

please	bitte	*bit-eh*
thank you (kindly)	danke (schön)	*dahnk-eh (shern)*
you're welcome	bitte (schön)	*bit-eh (shern)*
excuse me	Entschuldigung	*ent-shul-dig-ung*
excuse me	Verzeihung	*feh(r)-tsy-ung*

Culture note—Many thanks

There are various ways to say please and thank you in German, building on the basic *bitte* and *danke* with additional vocabulary. I always have to smile when I remember a version I was exposed to as a young teenager. I was devouring an outdated European travel guide (Fodors or Frommers), and the Germany section instructed readers to thank in German by saying *Danke vielmals* ("thank you very much"), which should be pronounced "donkey fieldmouse." You can try "donkey fieldmouse" if you want, or maybe *dahnk-eh feel-mahls*, if you want to be a little more accurate.

Culture note—Gestures

Beware of using gestures abroad, because they often mean something unexpected. For example, in the U.S., we might tap our forehead with an index finger to denote "good thinking" or to indicate that someone is intelligent. In Germany and Austria, this same gesture means that you think someone is crazy.

You should also avoid the OK sign (thumb and index finger forming a circle), as some people consider it vulgar. If you want to wish someone good luck, don't cross your fingers; tuck your thumb inside your other fingers and form a fist. Thumbs up and thumbs down are popular gestures for indicating approval, satisfaction, and happiness or, pointing down, the opposite.

Lodging

If you are arranging your own lodging, you should be familiar with the vocabulary in this section. Even if your lodging will be arranged for you, you will find some of these words and phrases useful.

where?	wo?	*voh?*
Where is ___, please?	Wo ist ___, bitte?	*voh ist ___, <u>bit</u>-eh?*
the hotel	das Hotel	*dahs hoh-<u>tel</u>*
the guesthouse, B&B	die Pension	*dee pen-<u>zyohn</u>*
here	hier	*hee(r)*
there	da	*dah*
Go ___.	Gehen Sie ___!	*<u>gay</u>-en zee ___!*
right	rechts	*Re^{ch}ts*
left	links	*links*
straight	geradeaus	*geh-Rah-deh-<u>ows</u>*
"always straight" = keep going straight	immer geradeaus	*<u>im</u>-eh(r) geh-Rah-deh-<u>ows</u>*
back	zurück	*tsoo-<u>Rewk</u>*
then	dann	*dahn*
Stop ___.	Halten Sie ___!	*<u>hahl</u>-ten zee ___!*
Can you___?	Können Sie___?	*<u>ker</u>-nen zee ___?*
to recommend	empfehlen	*em-<u>pfay</u>-len*
Can you recommend ___?	Können Sie ___empfehlen?	*<u>ker</u>-nen zee ___ em-<u>pfay</u>-len?*
a hotel	ein Hotel	*ine hoh-<u>tel</u>*
a guesthouse	eine Pension	*<u>ine</u>-eh pen-<u>zyohn</u>*
reservation	die Reservierung	*dee Reh-zeh(r)-<u>veeR</u>-ung*
I have ___.	Ich habe ___.	*i^{ch} <u>hah</u>-beh ___*
I have a reservation.	Ich habe eine Reservierung.	*i^{ch} <u>hah</u>-beh <u>ine</u>-eh Reh-zeh(r)-<u>veeR</u>-ung*
room	das Zimmer	*dahs <u>tsim</u>-eh(r)*

free, available	frei	*fRy*
Do you have ___?	Haben Sie ___?	*hah-ben zee ___?*
Do you have rooms available?	Haben Sie Zimmer frei?	*hah-ben zee tsim-meh(r) fRy?*
I would like ___.	Ich möchte ___.	*i^{ch} mer^{ch}-teh ___*
a double room	ein Doppelzimmer	*ine dop-el-tsim-eh(r)*
a single room	ein Einzelzimmer	*ine ine-tsel-tsim-eh(r)*
with shower	mit Dusche	*mit doo-sheh*
with bath	mit Bad	*mit baht*
for one night	für eine Nacht	*few(r) ine-eh nah_{ch}t*
for __(3)__ nights	für __(3)__ Nächte	*few(r) (dRy) neh^{ch}-teh*

Example: Ich möchte ein Doppelzimmer mit Bad für zwei Nächte.

Culture note—Showers and water temperature

A German or Austrian shower typically has a narrow shower head with a metal hose running to it, and the head can be detached from the shower head base and held in the hand. In fact, sometimes the "shower" may look like a bathtub to you, but because of the removable shower head, it is still considered a shower. Just one of the everyday differences that make travel interesting.

Whether you have a bath or shower at your disposal, make sure you set the water temperature before stepping in. Hot water can be scaldingly hot. Be careful not to burn yourself.

---

from. . . to	von. . . bis	*fon. . . bis*
from Saturday to Monday	von Samstag bis Montag	*fon zahm-stahk bis mohn-tahk*
how much?	wieviel?	*vee-feel?*
to cost	kosten	*kos-ten*
that	das	*dahs*
it	es	*es*
How much does that cost, please?	Wieviel kostet das, bitte?	*vee-feel kos-tet dahs, bit-eh?*

Culture note—Hotel forms

You may need to complete a registration form at your hotel. If you are asked to produce identification and write down an ID number, you can use your passport. When you write dates, such as your birth date or check-in/check-out dates, remember to write the date, then the month, then the year. (It's easy to forget.)

How much does a double room cost?	Wieviel kostet ein Doppelzimmer?	*vee-feel kos-tet ine dop-el tsim-eh(r)?*
with	mit	*mit*
without	ohne	*oh-neh*
breakfast	das Frühstück	*dahs fRew-shtewk*
Is that with breakfast?	Ist das mit Frühstück?	*ist dahs mit fRew-shtewk?*
How much does that cost with breakfast?	Wieviel kostet das mit Frühstück?	*vee-feel kos-tet dahs mit fRew-shtewk?*
Could I see the room, please?	Könnte ich das Zimmer sehen, bitte?	*kern-teh i^{ch} dahs tsim-eh(r) zay-en, bit-eh?*
I'll take it.	Ich nehme es.	*i^{ch} nay-meh es*
I won't take it.	Ich nehme es nicht.	*i^{ch} nay-meh es ni^{ch}t*
too	zu	*tsoo*
expensive	teuer	*toy-eh(r)*
cheap	billig	*bil-i^{ch}*
cheaper	billiger	*bil-i^{ch}-eh(r)*
economical	preisgünstig	*pRice-gewn-sti^{ch}*
something	etwas	*et-vahs*
something ___-er	etwas ___+es	*et-vahs ___-es*
something cheaper	etwas Billigeres	*et-vahs bil-i^{ch}-eh(r)-es*
Do you have something ___?	Haben Sie etwas ___+es?	*hah-ben zee et-vahs ___-es?*
receipt	die Quittung	*dee kvit-ung*
key	der Schlüssel	*day(r) shlew-sel*

Exercise 2.6

Translate into German.

1. Where is the *Hotel Tannenbaum*, please?

2. Excuse me. Can you recommend a guesthouse?

3. Do you have rooms available?

4. I would like a double room with a bath for one night.

5. I would like a single room with a shower. For three nights. From Sunday to Wednesday.

6. How much does that cost?

7. How much does a double room cost?

8. Is that with breakfast?

9. How much does that cost without breakfast?

10. I'll take it.

11. That is too expensive.

12. Do you have something cheaper? *

13. I would like a receipt, please.

14. Where is the key?

15. That's very economical/well priced!

16. I have a reservation.

Answers: 1) Wo ist das Hotel Tannenbaum, bitte? 2) Entschuldigung (or variation)! Können Sie eine Pension empfehlen? 3) Haben Sie Zimmer frei? 4) Ich möchte ein Doppelzimmer mit Bad für eine Nacht. 5) Ich möchte ein Einzelzimmer mit Dusche. Für drei Nächte. Von Sonntag bis Mittwoch. 6) Wieviel kostet das? 7) Wieviel kostet ein Doppelzimmer? 8) Ist das mit Frühstück? 9) Wieviel kostet das ohne Frühstück? 10) Ich nehme es. 11) Das ist zu teuer. 12) Haben Sie etwas Billigeres*? 13) Ich möchte eine Quittung, bitte. 14) Wo ist der Schlüssel? 15) Das ist sehr preisgünstig! 16) Ich habe eine Reservierung.

* Grammar quirk: When saying "something ___" in German, such as "something cheaper," you need to add an *-es* to the end of the descriptive word and capitalize the first letter, such as when you build on the word *billig* to get "etwas Billigeres."

Culture note—Mini-bars

Beware the hotel mini-bar! That enticing basket of snacks or fridge stocked with drinks is going to be as overpriced as the mini-bar in an American hotel. Even worse, if the dollar is weak. Try to keep a few snacks with you as you travel, so you are less likely to run up a tab on the hotel room snacks.

Culture note—Window shades, levers and screens

Most homes and some hotels will have heavy exterior shades to lower on the windows, shutting out light and possibly some of the exterior noise. To close your *Rollladen* (or *Rolladen*, with old spelling), grasp the broad cloth band or cord firmly, pull out at the bottom while holding the top steady, and slowly lower the heavy shade. Pulling the shade up in the morning is easy—just pull down on the cord or band to lift the shade, and the band should retract back into its holder on its own. I know, this sounds obvious, but it can happen that you somehow snarl the cord up, if you don't use it properly.

Many hotel rooms have the same type of "convertible" window popular in most homes—turn the handle one way, and the window stays firmly shut, turn it another way, and you can tip the top open, turn it another way, and the whole window swings open. When changing from one setting to another, make sure to close the window completely between "tip" and "wide open." I know I'm not the only American who has changed settings in a hurry and ended up wrestling to reattach a large, heavy window that is hanging by one corner instead of two.

And what about window screens? They are so rare that one might be tempted to say they don't exist in Germany or Austria. There seem to be fewer flying critters than many of us have at home. Also, the heavy window shades function to keep flying things out at night. And lastly, with windows in the "tip" position overnight rather than "wide open," there's less likelihood that night creatures will invade your room to begin with.

Important words

where?	wo?	*voh?*
where from?	woher?	*voh-hay(r)?*
where to?	wohin?	*voh-hin?*
here	hier	*hee(r)*
there	da	*dah*
what?	was?	*vahs?*
that	das	*dahs*
who?	wer?	*vay(r)?*
when?	wann?	*vahn?*
how long?	wie lange?	*vee lang-eh?*
why?	warum?	*vah-Room?*
how?	wie?	*vee?*
how much?	wieviel?	*vee-feel?*
how many?	wie viele?	*vee feel-eh?*

Exercise 2.7
Find the answers to these questions.

1. Was ist das?
2. Wer sind Sie?

3. Wieviel kostet das Zimmer?
4. Wie lange sind Sie in Berlin?
5. Wie fahren Sie?
6. Woher kommen Sie?
7. Wie viele Leute (people) sind das?
8. Wohin fahren Sie?
9. Wo wohnen Sie in Amerika?

A. Ich bin Martin Hausmann.
B. Das sind zwei Männer und drei Frauen.
C. Wir fahren mit dem Auto.

D. Ich wohne in Kalifornien.

E. Das ist ein Federbett.
F. Ich bin vier Tage hier.
G. Wir fahren nach Salzburg.

H. Ich komme aus der USA.
I. Es kostet 60 Euro.

Answers: 1) E, 2) A, 3) I, 4) F, 5) C, 6) H, 7) B, 8) G, 9) D

Culture note—Hotel customs

Unless you stay in a mid-range or higher hotel (three stars or more), your lodging may not have many "American" amenities. If you are staying in budget accommodations, bring your own soap, shampoo and washcloth. Even higher-end hotels usually do not offer washcloths. (If you want, you can purchase inexpensive disposable washcloths—*Einweg-Waschlappen* or *Einmal-Waschlappen*—from a drugstore or supermarket, where a package of 100 won't cost more than a couple of euros. Look in the area that sells toilet paper and facial tissues.) If you are in lower-priced lodging, don't expect to have a private bathroom without checking to see whether it's included (and it will cost more). If you have a room without a private bath, you will have access to a shared bathroom.

Not surprisingly, environmental concerns have entered the hotel business in Germany and Austria. Your bathroom will probably have a sign noting that because of "Umweltschutz" (environmental protection), towels are replaced only if you leave them on the floor. Most hotels request that you use towels more than one day in order to conserve the water and energy used in washing them.

The hotel bill includes a service charge. There's no need to tip, unless you get special service from someone. If you want to be especially polite and gracious, you may leave a small tip for the chambermaid on your pillow, but most locals don't follow this practice. Breakfast (*Frühstück*) is usually included in the price, but you should check this when you agree to take a room.

A cause of much confusion: The system for numbering floors differs in Europe and the United States. A European first floor is an American second floor, etc. In German, the first floor is called the *Erdgeschoß* (ground floor). In German, the second floor is called the *1. Stock* or *Etage*, and the third floor is the *2. Stock* or *Etage*. Just remember to add *one* to whatever German floor number you are told to go to, and you will get to the right floor. If you have an elevator in your hotel, realize that the main floor will be identified by an E or possibly a 0, not the 1 you are probably used to.

Culture note—Günstig

A useful word to know in Germany and Austria is *günstig* (<u>gewn</u>-*sti*^{ch}), which means favorable, beneficial, reasonable. It's *günstig* to know the word *günstig*, as the word comes in handy a lot. A favorable exchange rate is *günstig*. You want to know which hotel is *günstiger?* One could be better than another because of cost or location or amenities. Which route is *günstiger?* Which schedule of activities for the next day? Whichever choice is better is *günstiger*. If you think something is a good deal or otherwise favorable, impress the locals and say that it's *günstig*.

---

3   Restaurants and Food

Numbers (11-20)

Time to tackle more numbers. First, review the numbers zero through ten.

Now take a look at eleven through twenty. (Practice saying them out loud.)

11	elf	*elf*
12	zwölf	*tsverlf*
13	dreizehn	*dRy-tsayn*
14	vierzehn	*fee(r)-tsayn*
15	fünfzehn	*fewnf-tsayn*
16	sechzehn	*ze^{ch}-tsayn*
17	siebzehn	*zeep-tsayn*
18	achtzehn	*ah$_{ch}$-tsayn*
19	neunzehn	*noyn-tsayn*
20	zwanzig	*tsvahn-tsi^{ch}*

Exercise 3.1

Translate the following numbers into German. Try not to look at the list above.

eleven	eighteen
sixteen	fourteen
twelve	nineteen
seventeen	fifteen
thirteen	twenty

Culture note—Ruhetag

Most restaurants, museums and galleries will close for one day a week, called *Ruhetag* (day of rest). The most common day for *Ruhetag* is Monday, although it can be any day of the week. You can check a place's posted hours to see when it has *Ruhetag*.

Exercise 3.2
Try some more advanced math.

1. zwölf plus fünf =

2. achtzehn plus zwei =

3. sieben plus sechs =

4. neunzehn minus drei =

5. zehn plus eins =

6. elf plus acht =

7. siebzehn minus zwei =

8. sechzehn minus vier =

9. neun plus neun =

10. acht plus sechs =

Answers: 1) siebzehn, 2) zwanzig, 3) dreizehn, 4) sechzehn, 5) elf, 6) neunzehn,
7) fünfzehn, 8) zwölf, 9) achtzehn, 10) vierzehn

Places to Eat

das Gasthaus	inn, home-style cooking
die Gaststätte	restaurant
das Restaurant	restaurant (fancier)
die Bierhalle	beer hall, offers basic food
die Bierstube	pub, limited food selection
der Schnellimbiß	snack bar, traditional fast food
das Café	coffee shop, with pastries
die Konditorei	pastry shop, has coffee

Travel tip: My brother-in-law is an avid traveler to Germany and enthusiastically tries the regional specialties. He recommends locating a restaurant that claims to have *Gutbürgerliche Küche* (good plain cooking) if you want to find someplace where you can eat traditional hearty food.

Food

Food is an integral part of any culture, with so many variations that we could easily have a shelf of books just on German and Austrian cuisine. Here is a summary of the most common or important food words, to give you a taste of what to expect.

Reality check: Because there are so many food words, it's hard to learn them all, especially if you haven't actually eaten the items. Don't worry about memorizing lists of food, if you are short on time. There's not really any need to. Take a phrase book or small dictionary with you, and you can look up enough to find out whether you are about to order a pork tenderloin or fried calf's brains.

It makes sense to learn a few basic words for drinks you like and for basic foods you know you like (beef, chicken, potatoes), but don't waste precious study time on vocabulary that you will have time to look up when you need it. You will be better off concentrating on main phrases and cultural information, so you will feel comfortable entering a restaurant, ordering, eating and paying.

Meals

breakfast	das Frühstück	*dahs <u>fRew</u>-shtewk*
lunch	das Mittagessen	*dahs <u>mit</u>-tahg-es-en*
afternoon coffee	der Kaffee	*day(r) kah-fay*
supper	das Abendessen	*dahs <u>ah</u>-bent-es-en*
light supper of sandwiches	das Abendbrot	*dahs <u>ah</u>-bent-bRoht*

Culture note—Organics

Germans and Austrians are big supporters and consumers of organic food. The magic term in German is "Bio," pronounced <u>bee</u>-oh. Or if you see "Natur" in front of something, like *Natur-kost* (natural food), then the emphasis is also on naturalness and health.

Culture note—Entering a restaurant

If you are in the south, you might say *Guten Tag/Abend!* or *Grüß Gott!* to the room at large when you enter a restaurant. (Locals might knock on tables as they pass, as a greeting. Don't be alarmed if this happens.) You generally seat yourself. It's a common practice, especially in the south, for parties to share tables if none are vacant.

One table to avoid in any pub is the *Stammtisch*, which is reserved for regular customers. The *Stammtisch* is usually marked by a sign or an elaborate ashtray and is probably a round table. Locals join each other at the *Stammtisch* to drink, argue and play cards.

Ordering

Waiter!/Waitress!	Entschuldigung, bitte!	ent-<u>shul</u>-dig-ung, <u>bit</u>-eh
Ready?	Fertig?	<u>feh(r)</u>-ti^{ch}?
What would you like?	Was hätten Sie gern?	vahs <u>het</u>-en zee geh(r)n?
	Was möchten Sie?	vahs <u>mer</u>^{ch}-ten zee?
to order	bestellen	beh-<u>shtel</u>-en
We would like ___.	Wir möchten ___.	vee(r) <u>mer</u>^{ch}-ten ___
We would like to order.	Wir möchten bestellen.	vee(r) <u>mer</u>^{ch}-ten beh-<u>shtel</u>-en
I would like to order.	Ich möchte bestellen.	i^{ch} <u>mer</u>^{ch}-teh beh-<u>shtel</u>-en
to recommend	empfehlen	em-<u>pfay</u>-len
Can you ___?	Können Sie ___?	<u>kern</u>-en zee ___?
Can you recommend ___?	Können Sie ___ empfehlen?	<u>kern</u>-en zee ___ em-<u>pfay</u>-len?
something	etwas	<u>et</u>-vahs
an inn	ein Gasthaus	ine <u>gahst</u>-hows
Do you have ___?	Haben Sie ___?	<u>hah</u>-ben zee ___?
children's portions	Kinderportionen	<u>kin</u>-deh(r)-po(r)-tsyohn-en
Wiener schnitzel	Wiener Schnitzel	<u>vee</u>-neh(r) <u>shnit</u>-sel
goulash soup	Gulaschsuppe	<u>goo</u>-lahsh-zup-eh

I would like ___.	Ich möchte ___.	i^{ch} _mer^{ch}-teh_ ___
a beer	ein Bier	_ine bee(r)_
a mineral water	ein Mineralwasser	_ine min-eh-Rahl-wah-seh(r)_
tomato soup	Tomatensuppe	_toh-mah-ten-zup-eh_
I like to eat/drink ___.	Ich esse/trinke gern ___.	i^{ch} _es-eh/tRink-eh geh(r)n_ ___
I don't like to eat/drink ___.	Ich esse/trinke nicht gern ___.	i^{ch} _es-eh/tRink-eh ni^{ch}t geh(r)n_ ___
I like to eat that.	Ich esse das gern.	i^{ch} _es-eh dahs geh(r)n_
I don't like to eat that.	Ich esse das nicht gern.	i^{ch} _es-eh dahs ni^{ch}t geh(r)n_

Travel tip: A college professor friend likes to try the house specialties when he travels. If this interests you, also, you can ask, *Was ist die Hausspezialität?* [*vahs ist dee hows-shpet-see-ah-lee-tayt?*]

Culture note—*Guten Appetit!*

Before you start eating a meal, it is polite to wish your fellow diners *Guten Appetit!* (in Germany) or *Mahlzeit!* (in Austria). The closest equivalent to these that we have in English is "Enjoy your meal."

Similarly, before drinking with others, it is polite to say *Prost!* (Cheers!) or *Zum Wohl!* (To your health!). The former is more down-to-earth, the latter somewhat more refined. You might be more likely to say *Prost* with beer and *Zum Wohl* with wine, but usage varies.

To toast, you hold your glass up, say your toast, take a drink, then hold your glass up again. You may or may not clink glasses. Try to maintain lots of eye contact.

In general, you should not eat or drink until everyone at your table has been served. The exception is with large groups, but even then, you might wait if your food won't grow cold in the process.

Culture note—Daily menu

Many places will have a set meal for a fixed price (often a daily special) identified as the *Tagesmenü*. The special or *Menü* will often be advertised (handwritten) on a blackboard in front of a restaurant. These specials are generally a good deal, although there won't be many choices available. For many weary travelers, limited options are just fine. Be aware: the word *Menü* in German means a set-price meal. The term for menu, listing all that the establishment offers, is *die Speisekarte*.

The Menu

menu	die Speisekarte	*dee shpy-zeh-kah(r)-teh*
appetizers	Vorspeisen	*foh(r)-shpy-zen*
soups	Suppen	*zup-en*
salads	Salate	*zah-lah-teh*
meat dishes	Fleischgerichte	*flysh-geh-Ri ch-teh*
fish dishes	Fischgerichte	*fish-geh-Ri ch-teh*
fowl	Geflügel	*geh-flew-gehl*
game	Wild	*vilt*
vegetables	Gemüse	*geh-mew-zeh*
cheese	Käse	*kay-zeh*
desserts	Nachspeisen	*nah ch-shpy-zen*

Culture note—Ordering beverages

Ein Bier, zwei Bier, drei Bier—When you order glasses of beer, you always say that you want so many "Bier," not "Biers," regardless of how many. The same rule can apply if you are ordering glasses of soda, juice, or whatever: *drei Apfelsaft, bitte; zwei Kola, bitte*. If ordering wine, you could use the same technique or specify an amount and color of wine: *zwei Achtel Rot, bitte* (2 one-eighth-liter glasses of red), *ein Viertel Weiß* (¼ liter of white).

Drinks

drinks	die Getränke	*dee geh-<u>tRenk</u>-eh*
water	das Wasser	*dahs <u>vahs</u>-eh(r)*
tap water	das Leitungswasser	*dahs <u>ly</u>-tungs-vahs-eh(r)*
mineral water	das Mineralwasser	*dahs min-eh-<u>Rahl</u>-vahs-eh(r)*
non-carbonated	still	*shtil*
drinkable water	das Trinkwasser	*dahs <u>tRink</u>-vahs-eh(r)*
warning: not drinkable	Kein Trinkwasser!	*kine <u>tRink</u>-vahs-eh(r)*
beer	das Bier	*dahs bee(r)*
wine	der Wein	*day(r) vine*
red wine	der Rotwein	*day(r) <u>Roht</u>-vine*
white wine	der Weißwein	*day(r) <u>vice</u>-vine*
the wine list	die Weinliste	*dee <u>vine</u>-list-eh*
a glass of ____	ein Glas ____	*ine glahs ____*
a bottle of ____	eine Flasche ____	*<u>ine</u>-eh <u>flahsh</u>-eh ____*
a cup of ____	eine Tasse ____	*<u>ine</u>-eh <u>tahs</u>-eh ____*
a small pot of ____	ein Kännchen ____	*ine <u>ken</u>-*^{*ch*}*en ____*
tea	der Tee	*day(r) tay*
coffee	der Kaffee	*day(r) kah-fay*
soda pop	die Limonade	*dee lee-moh-<u>nah</u>-deh*
cola	die Cola	*dee <u>koh</u>-lah*
juice	der Saft	*day(r) zahft*
milk	die Milch	*dee mil*^{*ch*}

Culture note—Mineral water

Most people drink lots of bottled mineral water, and it's usually carbonated. Different ways of indicating carbonation are *mit Gas*, *mit Kohlensäure* (with carbonation), *sprudelnd* (sparkling), and *prickelnd* ("tingly"). A less heavily carbonated mineral water that still contains bubbles is *mild*. Locals drink their mineral water straight or use it to dilute fruit juices or wine.

Culture note—Drinking water

German restaurant workers do not automatically place water on the table for customers to drink. If you want water, you must ask for it. If you ask for *Ein Glas Wasser, bitte*, the waitperson will probably bring you a glass or bottle of sparkling mineral water, and you will pay for it. If you want bottled, non-carbonated water, ask for water *ohne Kohlensäure* or *stilles Wasser*. If you particularly want tap water, you should ask for *Leitungswasser*. The tap water in Germany, Switzerland and Austria is perfectly safe to drink. Be aware, however, that locals will likely think that drinking tap water as a beverage is a little odd. And as with other cool drinks, water will usually not be served with ice. You may be able to receive ice upon request (*Mit Eiswürfeln, bitte.*), but you are fighting a losing battle. Consider giving in and drinking cool rather than ice cold beverages during your stay.

Culture note—Meal beverage customs

During meals, Germans drink wine, beer, mineral water or juice. In general, adults do not drink milk, viewing it as a beverage for children.

Other than breakfast and afternoon coffee, Germans and Austrians do not drink coffee at their meals, perhaps because the coffee is important enough to be savored on its own. You may have heard about the strength of European coffee. It is strong, but very flavorful. If you don't particularly like coffee but want to join in the custom, load it up with sugar and cream and make it a real treat. Just don't drink too much, if you are sensitive to caffeine. You can get decaffeinated coffee in coffee shops (order *koffeinfrei* or *ohne Koffein*), but most homes will not have decaf on hand.

It's quite easy to get tea, if that is your preferred drink. Both herbal tea (*Kräutertee*) and black tea (*schwarzer Tee*) are readily available.

Culture note—Soft drinks

While glasses of beer can seem quite generous in Germany and Austria, the soft drink servings will be small by American standards, and it's very unlikely that there will be any free refills (for coffee, either, by the way). You really get much more beer for your money than most other beverages.

Breakfast

egg	das Ei	*dahs eye*
cheese	der Käse	*day(r) kay-zeh*
assorted cold cuts	der Aufschnitt	*day(r) owf-shnit*
cheese spread	der Streichkäse	*day(r) shtRy^ch-kay-zeh*
bread	das Brot	*dahs bRoht*
roll	das Brötchen	*dahs bRert-^chen*
	die Semmel	*dee zem-el*
toast	der Toast	*day(r) tohst*
butter	die Butter	*dee but-eh(r)*
jam	die Marmelade	*dee mah(r)-may-lah-deh*
honey	der Honig	*day(r) hoh-ni^ch*
cereal	die Getreideflocken	*dee geh-tRy-deh-flok-en*
juice	der Saft	*day(r) zahft*
sugar	der Zucker	*day(r) tsuk-eh(r)*
cream	die Sahne	*dee zah-neh*

Culture note—Tabletop trash container

Your breakfast table might include a cylindrical plastic container (typically about the size of a small coffee can) for breakfast refuse. Use it for throwing away your egg shells, plastic jam containers, tea bags, butter wrappings—any breakfast debris you want to dispose of. Don't use the container as a general garbage can, though. You shouldn't clean all the junk out of your tote bag and stuff it in.

Culture note—Juice

A much wider range of juices is drunk abroad than is typical in the United States, and not just for breakfast. Apple juice, orange (often without the pulp), cherry, grape and pineapple are all common, along with more exotic tropical combinations. "Mineral" juice—fortified with minerals—is also popular. Many people prefer to dilute their juice with mineral water.

Culture note—Typical breakfast

At most places, breakfast is continental. Most hotels now offer a buffet breakfast, but smaller or more traditional establishments may still bring your party's breakfast to your table.

The bare essentials for breakfast are rolls, jam and coffee or tea (you order one or the other). Children will usually be offered hot chocolate. You will almost always get a plate with cold cuts and/or cheese slices or cheese spread. You may get a soft-boiled egg in an egg cup. (Chop off the top, or crack the shell and peel it off the top, and eat the egg out of the shell using the little spoon that comes with it.) Yogurt and a couple types of dry cereal are common offerings. You might get orange juice or some other fruit drink, but not always.

You can always request more than the standard breakfast provided by your pension or hotel (an egg, for example), often at no extra charge. (This is something you can ask about, though, if you don't want to pay more.) If dry cereals are available, probably on a table somewhere, then there's likely a pitcher of milk there, too. The milk may not be cold.

If you have a breakfast buffet, you are not supposed to pack up extra rolls with meat and cheese and take them along for your lunch. This is inconsiderate and will irritate the hotel owners, who agreed to supply your breakfast, not additional meals.

Culture note—A roll by any other name

Standard white-bread breakfast rolls (also eaten at other times of the day) are generally called *Brötchen* in Germany and are oval, and are called *Semmeln* in Austria, where they are round with a pinwheel pattern on top. There are occasional other variants—such as *Schrippen* in and near Berlin—but *Brötchen/Semmeln* should carry you through your trip just fine.

Locals take a knife and saw through the roll (or cut a slit in the side, stick their thumbs in the opening and tear the roll apart), making a top half and a bottom half. At a buffet, there might be a bread knife in the bread basket for that purpose. They typically eat the rolls with butter, meat and cheese for breakfast, although jams are also available. Most people eat each half of the roll separate, as an open-faced sandwich, using their hands.

It's unusual for sweet rolls or muffins to make an appearance at the breakfast table, but you might see some at a breakfast buffet.

Soup

liver-dumpling soup	die Leberknödel-suppe	dee _lay_-beh(r)-kner-del-zup-eh
spiced soup of stewed beef	die Gulaschsuppe	dee _goo_-lahsh-zup-eh
onion soup	die Zwiebelsuppe	dee _tsvee_-bel-zup-eh
tomato soup	die Tomatensuppe	dee toh-_mah_-ten-zup-eh
lentil soup	die Linsensuppe	dee _lin_-zen-zup-eh
pea soup	die Erbsensuppe	dee _eh(r)p_-sen-zup-eh
oxtail soup	die Ochsen-schwanzsuppe	dee _ok_-sen-shvahnts-zup-eh
clear soup with pancake strips	die Frittatensuppe	dee fʀi-_tah_-ten-zup-eh
soup of the day	die Tagessuppe	dee _tahg_-es-zup-eh

Culture note—The main meal

Traditionally, lunch is the main meal in Germany and Austria. It is usually hot and filling. With so many people working away from home, though, this custom is changing, and for many now, the main meal is in the evening. Still, many families eat only one warm meal a day, filling in the other with open-faced sandwiches, fruits and vegetables. Dessert is not part of the traditional German or Austrian meal.

Supper can be a light affair for those who ate a large lunch, or a heavier meal, if it is the main meal of the day. Traditionally, *das Abendessen* consists of open-faced sandwiches of meat and cheese, in which case it may be called *Abendbrot*.

Meat, Poultry, Game and Fish

beef	das Rindfleisch	*dahs Rint-flysh*
pork	das Schweinefleisch	*dahs shvine-eh-flysh*
ham	der Schinken	*day(r) shink-en*
bacon	der Speck	*day(r) shpek*
pork chop	das Schweinekotelett	*dahs shvine-eh-koht-let*
schnitzel	das Schnitzel	*dahs shnit-sel*
veal	das Kalbfleisch	*dahs kahlp-flysh*
meat patties	die Frikadellen	*dee fRik-ah-del-en*
sausage	die Wurst	*dee vu(r)st*
bratwurst	die Bratwurst	*dee bRaht-vu(r)st*
hot dog	das Wiener Würstchen	*dahs vee-neh(r) vu(r)st-^{ch}en*
	die Frankfurter	*dee fRahnk-fu(r)-teh(r)*
	die Würstel	*die vew(r)-stel*
blood sausage	die Blutwurst	*dee bloot-vu(r)st*
chicken	das Huhn	*dahs hoon*
	das Hühnchen	*dahs hewn-^{ch}en*
	das Hähnchen	*dahs hen-^{ch}en*
	das Hendl	*dahs hendl*

turkey	der Truthahn	*day(r) tRoot-hahn*
	der Puter	*day(r) poo-teh(r)*
venison	das Reh	*dahs Ray*
fish	der Fisch	*day(r) fish*
tuna	der Thunfisch	*day(r) toon-fish*
trout	die Forelle	*dee foh(r)-el-eh*
salmon	der Lachs	*day(r) la_{ch}s*

Culture note—Hot dogs

In Germany, hot dogs are called *Wiener Würstchen* (wieners, presumably named after Vienna, Austria), but in Austria, they're called *Frankfurter* (frankfurters, named after Frankfurt, Germany). Whatever you call your hot dog, you're generally supposed to grasp the sausage and eat it with your fingers, not a knife and fork. You can usually order ketchup or mustard to go along with it.

A "Hotdog" in German, by the way, refers to the sausage and a surrounding bun together. If you ask for a Hotdog at a typical snack shop, they might tell you they don't have Hotdogs, even though they sell *Frankfurter* or *Wiener Würstchen*. If it doesn't come in a bun, it's not a Hotdog, and most of them don't come in a bun, although they might have a hard roll on the side.

Some sausage types, such as Munich's *Weißwurst*, have a tough skin that is typically not eaten. People either slit the sausage open, eat the center out of it, then don't eat the skin, or else peel the skin down and eat out the soft center.

Starches

potato	die Kartoffel	*dee kah(r)-tof-el*
	der Erdapfel	*day(r) ay(r)t-ahp-fel*
rice	der Reis	*day(r) Rice*
noodles	die Nudeln	*dee noo-deln*
tiny flour dumplings	die Spätzle	*dee shpets-leh*
dumpling	der Knödel	*day(r) kner-del*
	der Kloß	*day(r) klohs*
French fries	die Pommes frites	*dee pom fRit*

Culture note—Potatoes and other soft foods

Potatoes are a beloved side dish throughout many areas of Germany and Austria, often simple boiled potatoes with fresh parsley sprinkled on top, with no sauce, gravy, or butter.

Potatoes, like other soft foods such as eggs and cooked vegetables, are generally cut at the table with a fork. Using a knife to cut these items may mark you as a tourist and might even be considered ill-mannered. Regional and generational expectations vary on this practice, with Austria and young people being laxer than Germany and the older generation. To be honest, I didn't learn about this bit of etiquette until almost 25 *years* after my first visit to the German-speaking world. Dozens of people probably think I have terrible table manners, but no one ever said anything to me about this. I wish they had. It never crossed my mind that cutting my potatoes with a knife might be considered rude.

Vegetables and Salad

cabbage	das Kraut	*dahs kRowt*
	der Kohl	*day(r) kohl*
carrots	die Karotten	*dee kah-Rot-en*
	die Mohrrüben	*dee moh(r)-Rew-ben*
beans	die Bohnen	*dee boh-nen*
corn	der Mais	*day(r) mice*
mushrooms	die Pilze	*dee pil-tseh*
asparagus	der Spargel	*day(r) shpah(r)-gehl*
peas	die Erbsen	*dee eh(r)p-sen*
spinach	der Spinat	*day(r) shpin-aht*
lettuce	der grüne Salat	*day(r) gRew-neh zah-laht*
mixed salad	der gemischte Salat	*day(r) geh-mish-teh zah-laht*
tomato	die Tomate	*dee toh-mah-teh*
cucumber	die Gurke	*dee gu(r)-keh*
onion	die Zwiebel	*dee tsvee-bel*
cauliflower	der Blumenkohl	*day(r) bloo-men-kohl*

Culture note—Salads and dressing

German salads are becoming more "Americanized." A "mixed salad" used to consist of, say, a pile of shredded carrots, a pile of cucumber slices, a little pile of kidney beans, maybe a few bits of lettuce, a couple of tomato slices, some corn—a real "mix" of salads, usually doused heavily with vinegar and oil. Anymore you are just as likely to receive a lettuce-based salad, possibly with some of the other traditional offerings, and the house dressing could be something like ranch. If you want dressing on the side, you could try *"Das Dressing extra, bitte,"* but no promises, here.

Fruit

fruit	das Obst	*dahs ohpst*
apple	der Apfel	*day(r) ahp-fel*
banana	die Banane	*dee bah-nah-neh*
orange	die Orange	*dee oh-Rahn-zheh*
	die Apfelsine	*dee ahp-fel-zee-neh*
pear	die Birne	*dee bee(r)-neh*
strawberries	die Erdbeeren	*dee ay(r)t-bayR-en*
raspberries	die Himbeeren	*dee him-bayR-en*
cherries	die Kirschen	*dee ki(r)sh-en*
peach	der Pfirsich	*day(r) pfi(r)-zi^{ch}*
grapes	die Trauben	*dee tRow-ben*
	die Weintrauben	*dee vine-tRow-ben*
lemon	die Zitrone	*dee tsi-tRohn-eh*

Seasoning

salt	das Salz	*dahs zahlts*
pepper	der Pfeffer	*day(r) pfef-eh(r)*
mustard	der Senf	*day(r) zenf*
ketchup	der Ketchup	*day(r) ket-chup*
mayonnaise	die Mayonnaise	*dee mah-yoh-nay-zeh*
vinegar	der Essig	*day(r) es-i^{ch}*
sugar	der Zucker	*day(r) tsuk-eh(r)*
honey	der Honig	*day(r) hoh-ni^{ch}*

Culture note—Pizza

German and Austrian pizza is quite different from American pizza. It tends to be Italian style—smaller, thinner, crisper, and not loaded down with toppings. Each person usually orders a separate pizza. Toppings are also different. You might have corn, tuna, artichokes, or hot dogs among your choices. While the toppings may not be what you expect, most of them are quite good. Go ahead—be daring!

Culture note—Kaffee

Kaffee (coffee) is almost its own meal, and it's in the afternoon. *Kaffee* is a fancier affair than the American morning coffee. *Kaffee* features cookies or cakes and, if in someone's home, nice china. Unlike lunch and supper, which usually do not end in a rich dessert, *Kaffee* is the time to indulge a sweet tooth. If you are invited to someone's home for *Kaffee*, rest assured that your hostess will pull out all the stops. Feel free to treat yourself equally well when you have *Kaffee* on your own in a Konditorei.

You may have noticed that when I include the word *Kaffee* in vocabulary lists, the pronunciation doesn't show which syllable should get the main stress, to be spoken more loudly. That's because most of Germany calls it <u>kah</u>-fay, but Austria calls it kah-<u>fay</u>. Both versions are good.

Culture note—Licking the coffee spoon

I can't get a straight answer on whether it's OK to lick off my coffee spoon in public. The coffee in a coffeehouse often has a frothy milk or cream topping, and I automatically want to pop the spoon into my mouth after I've stirred my sweetener into the brew. But the locals don't, at least not in public. At least not in Germany. But privately, yes. Well, some do, anyway. (The question has provoked heated disagreement between long-time spouses.) And in Austria? "Of course! We all do it!" There's too much variation to make a "manners" call on this one. Keep an eye on others and see what they do, if you want to fit in.

Dessert

cake	der Kuchen	day(r) koo-_ch_en
fancy cake	die Torte	dee toh(r)-teh
cookie	der Keks	day(r) kayks
	das Plätzchen	dahs plehts-_ch_en
apple strudel	der Apfelstrudel	day(r) ahp-fel-stRoo-del
ice cream	das Eis	dahs ice
chocolate	die Schokolade	dee shoh-koh-lah-deh
whipped cream	die Schlagsahne	dee shlahk-zah-neh
	das Schlagobers	dahs shlahk-oh-beh(r)s

Tableware

plate	der Teller	day(r) tel-eh(r)
glass	das Glas	dahs glahs
fork	die Gabel	dee gah-bel
knife	das Messer	dahs mes-eh(r)
spoon	der Löffel	day(r) lerf-el
napkin	die Serviette	dee zeh(r)-vyet-eh
to need	brauchen	bRow-_ch_en
I need ___.	Ich brauche ___.	i _ch_ bRow-_ch_eh ___

Culture note—Table manners

Germans generally hold their fork in the left hand, knife in the right, using the knife for cutting and for pushing food onto the fork. The knife and fork are also used for eating open-faced sandwiches. If you are using just one utensil, you should have it in your right hand and place your left hand on the table next to the plate, not on your lap. Contrary to the custom in the United States, it is considered bad manners to place a hand on the lap during a meal. It's also bad manners to switch your fork back and forth during a meal—keep it in the same hand. Other polite practices to aim for at the table include sitting up straight, keeping your elbows off the table, and putting your napkin on your lap. These are "good behavior" manners, though, and in informal situations, people routinely disregard them.

Culture note—Fingers or fork?

"Rules" for eating foods are often different in Germany and Austria than in the United States. Open-faced sandwiches— typical for supper and often breakfast—are usually eaten with a knife and fork. Toast is too hard to eat that way, though, and a white hard roll is too thick, so those are eaten in the hand. Dry cakes, such as pound cake, can be eaten in the hand, but moist cakes with a fork. In informal settings, hot dogs (without the bun) are generally held in the fingers when eaten.

And what if you don't know these practices or don't care to fol-low them? No big deal, but people might look at you curiously. I once disturbed a snack-bar proprietor by taking a knife and fork to eat my hot dog (no bun), but other than complaining to her husband, she didn't do anything. My Austrian lunch companions commented on it, though, because they knew I was interested in these types of differences.

Paying

to taste good	schmecken	*shmek-en*
Did it taste good?	Hat es geschmeckt?	*haht es geh-shmekt?*
Yes, it tasted good.	Ja, es hat gut geschmeckt! (Can shorten to Ja, gut!)	*yah, es haht goot geh-shmekt*
to pay	bezahlen	*beh-tsah-len*
= I'd like to pay.	Zahlen, bitte!	*tsah-len, bit-eh*
together	zusammen	*tsoo-zahm-en*
separate	getrennt	*geh-tRent*
Is that together?	Ist das zusammen?	*ist dahs tsoo-zahm-men?*
No, it's separate.	Nein, das ist getrennt. =separate checks	*nine, dahs ist geh-tRent*

Culture note—Paying, tipping and leaving

When you are done eating and want to leave, you usually need to indicate to the waiter or waitress that you are ready for the check. Try to catch their eye and call out, "Zahlen, bitte." The bill may be printed up already, or the waiter might add it up at your table, possibly even asking you what you ordered, if the place is informal and busy.

In Germany and Austria, you almost always pay for a meal or drinks at the table. Restaurants almost always include taxes and a service charge in their prices, but the usual custom is to round up a little when you pay your bill, unless you wish to show that you were unhappy with the service. Normally, for example, if your drinks cost 8 euros 60, you would round up to 9 or 10 euros.

Waitress: *Acht Euro sechzig.*
Customer: *Neun Euro, bitte.* (as you give her a ten)
Waitress: *Danke schön!* (while giving back one euro)

If you are more comfortable with a standard percentage, you could add an easy 10% to your bill as a tip. Unlike in America, it is not customary to leave a tip on the table, unless you paid with a credit card and the charge slip does not include space to add a tip. It's far more common to give the tip directly to the waiter or waitress. Another way to approach tipping is to indicate *how much you would like back*, and let the waiters or waitresses figure out their own tips.

Waiter: *Siebenundzwangiz Euro.* (27 euros)
Customer: *Ich möchte zwanzig zurück, bitte.* (as you give him a 50)
Waiter: *Vielen Dank!* (while giving back 20 euros)

Just as you might greet the room at large when you enter an eating establishment (depending on where you are), you might call *Auf Wiedersehen!* or *Auf Wiederschauen!* to the room at large when leaving.

Culture note—Es schmeckt!

You can get unbelievable mileage in terms of good will and gratitude with the short sentence *Es schmeckt* ("It tastes good."). At the end of a restaurant meal, the waitress will almost always ask, *Hat es geschmeckt?* ("Did it taste good?"), or some variation of that. The expected answer is something like, *Ja, es hat geschmeckt.* If you can produce an understandable response like that (or throw it out in German on your own, if the staff is using English with you), there's a good chance you can make your waitress swoon.

Think I'm joking? My husband and I were eating in a German restaurant after I had lived in Austria for most of a year. I had chatted comfortably and fluently with the waitress in German for several minutes at the end of our meal. Then she asked the pivotal question, *"Hat es geschmeckt?"* My husband answered in his best textbook German, *"Ja, es hat gut geschmeckt."* The waitress clutched her hands to her bosom, beaming with pleasure and crying out, *"Ach! Sie sprechen so gut Deutsch!"*

Five words. My husband got rhapsodized over because of those five magic words. My five minutes of fluent conversation had meant nothing. Gotta get *Es schmeckt* in there. Actually, there's a second lesson here—when you reach a certain level of fluency, people are a lot less likely to compliment you on your language or appreciate that effort is involved. So go ahead and make it clear that you are working hard—people will usually cut you more slack.

Exercise 3.3

How would you say the following in German?

1. Pardon me, please. Where is a *Gasthaus*?

2. Waiter! We would like to order.

3. I would like a mineral water, please. Non-carbonated.

4. Can you recommend something?

5. Do you have onion soup?

6. What is the soup of the day?

7. Can you recommend a beer?

8. I would like French fries.

9. I need a napkin, please.

10. It tasted good!

Answers: 1) Entschuldigung, bitte. Wo ist ein Gasthaus? 2) Entschuldigung, bitte. Wir möchten bestellen. 3) Ich möchte ein Mineralwasser, bitte. Ohne Gas./Still. 4) Können Sie etwas empfehlen? 5) Haben Sie Zwiebelsuppe? 6) Was ist die Tagessuppe? 7) Können Sie ein Bier empfehlen? 8) Ich möchte Pommes frites. 9) Ich brauche eine Serviette, bitte. 10) Es hat (gut) geschmeckt!

Culture note—Dinner rolls

In the south, if you find rolls, sliced bread or breadsticks in a basket on your table when you go somewhere to eat, you are free to eat them, but keep track of how many you have, because you will probably need to pay a small fee for each one. When your waiter comes to total up your bill, he will usually ask something about *Gebäck, Brot* or *Brötchen*, which is your cue to say how many pieces you had. You don't pay extra for rolls at breakfast, though, because they are the basis of the meal.

Exercise 3.4
Write several things that you like to eat or drink. For example, *Ich esse gern Wiener Schnitzel.*

1.
2.
3.
4.
5.

Answers: Ich esse gern ___./Ich trinke gern ___.

Now write what you *don't* like to eat or drink. For example, *Ich esse nicht gern Fisch.*

1.
2.
3.

Answers: Ich esse nicht gern ___./Ich trinke nicht gern ___.

Culture note—Buying fresh produce

If you buy fruits or vegetables in a grocery store, and they're not already packaged and marked with the price, you will need to weigh your purchase yourself, push the button on the scale for that particular fruit or vegetable, and print out your own label with the price for checking out. Checkout clerks don't weigh and price the produce; customers do.

Most Germans and Austrians are quite health conscious and strive to buy organic foods, known as "Bio" products. If some-one tells you the fruit or vegetable is "Bio," they are assuring you that it is pesticide-free and as healthy as possible.

Culture note—Smoking

Traditionally, smoking has been very popular in Germany and Austria, especially among young people. The smoking culture changed drastically in the mid-2000s, though, as both countries took steps to limit or prohibit public smoking.

So are the days of the smoke-shrouded coffeehouse over? Not exactly, at least as of this writing. Bans are often spotty and poorly enforced. But change is underway, and the situation has definitely improved. If you're a non-smoker, odds are you can find a public establishment that is acceptably smoke-free. Many restaurants will now have no-smoking sections. And if you're a smoker, keep your eyes out for what other patrons are doing and check whether ashtrays are on the tables before you light up, because public smoking is no longer the given it used to be in these countries.

4   Shopping and Sightseeing

Numbers (10-100, by ten)

Counting by tens isn't so bad in German. Review how to count from 0 to 20, then learn how to count to 100 by 10.

10	zehn	*tsayn*
20	zwanzig	*tsvahn-tsi^{ch}*
30	dreißig	*dRy-si^{ch}*
40	vierzig	*fee(r)-tsi^{ch}*
50	fünfzig	*fewnf-tsi^{ch}*
60	sechzig	*ze^{ch}-tsi^{ch}*
70	siebzig	*zeep-tsi^{ch}*
80	achtzig	*ah$_{ch}$-tsi^{ch}*
90	neunzig	*noyn-tsi^{ch}*
100	(ein)hundert	*(ine)-hun-deh(r)t*

Exercise 4.1

Translate the following numbers into German. Try not to look at the list above.

ten	eighty
sixty	forty
twenty	ninety
seventy	fifty
thirty	one hundred

Exercise 4.2

What is the answer in German?

1. Number of states in the United States
2. Two degrees below freezing (Fahrenheit)
3. Years in a century
4. Minimum age for an octogenarian
5. Number of cents in a dime

6. Common tax form—10??
7. Minutes in an hour
8. Degrees in a right angle
9. "Trombones in the big parade" (minus 6)
10. Start of the "roaring" decade

Answers: 1) fünfzig, 2) dreißig, 3) (ein)hundert, 4) achtzig, 5) zehn, 6) vierzig, 7) sechzig, 8) neunzig, 9) siebzig, 10) zwanzig

---

Culture note—Foot faux pas

No matter where you are—on a train, in a restaurant, in a home—you shouldn't put your feet on furniture if you're wearing shoes. Doing so is ill-mannered and highly frowned upon. On a train, the conductor will even say something to you if your shoes somehow come in contact with the seat. If you just have socks on your feet, then it is all right to place them on a chair, couch or bench. (Unless you are in a restaurant. Then it's still a no-no.)

Travel tip: Consider leaving at home something (or several things) you would like to have on your trip but can do without. This may motivate you to hunt for the items in German and Austrian stores, providing a dose of local life that you could easily miss if you don't need to shop for anything. And the experience is even better if you have to look through several shops and ask people for help. You are interacting with real locals, probably ones who don't work with tourists all day!

Or maybe set yourself a goal of finding something you want to bring back home—something "real life" and not touristy—and go for it. Do you like to cook? Check out the kitchen section of a department store. Or find a home-improvement center. Or a stationery store, or a music or book store—whatever interests you. Check out a real store and get a better sense of what real life is like in Germany or Austria. The experience will likely outweigh cramming one more church or museum into your schedule. Try something different!

Culture note—Credit cards

Use of credit cards is becoming increasingly common in Germany and Austria, though still not at the levels of use in the United States. Gas stations routinely take credit cards. Tourist hotels and trinket shops usually take credit cards. Many restaurants now accept credit cards. If you plan on using credit cards for most of your expenses, simply look at the window or door of an establishment before entering and see whether a sticker showing your type of credit card is posted. In general, the more expensive or touristy the business, the more likely it will accept credit cards. Mastercard and VISA are the brands most commonly allowed.

You will now be asked (or are supposed to be asked) whether you want to have the charge made in dollars (probably with less-favorable conversion rates and higher fees) or in euros (recommended by experts). Once you have chosen dollars or euros, you can't change your mind later, even if the exchange rate moves in a way you would like to take advantage of.

Grammar—Present tense verb endings

You already know the verb endings for *ich* and *Sie*. Now you will see that the verb form for *wir* (we) is exactly the same as the *Sie* form. You don't have to know the *wir* form to travel or visit successfully, but since it's basically a "freebie" (we get it "free" with the *Sie* form), you may as well take a look at it.

Subject	Verb Ending	Example
ich (I)	-e	ich komme
Sie (you)	-en	Sie kommen
wir (we)	-en	wir kommen

"Woher kommen Sie?"
"Ich komme aus Texas."
"Wir kommen aus Texas."

Exception to the verb-ending rule: *to be* (very irregular)

    ich bin   Sie sind   wir sind

But note, the *Sie* and *wir* forms are still identical.

Exercise 4.3

Answer the following questions. Practice both the *ich* form and the *wir* form.

1. Woher kommen Sie?

    Ich . . . .
    Wir . . . .

2. Wie heißen Sie?

    Ich . . . .
    Wir . . . .

3. Was essen Sie gern?

    Ich . . . .
    Wir . . . .

4. Was möchten Sie trinken?

    Ich . . . .
    Wir . . . .

5. Haben Sie eine Reservierung?

    Ja, ich . . . .
    Ja, wir . . . .

Answers: 1) Ich komme aus ___./Wir kommen aus ___. 2) Ich heiße ___./Wir heißen ___ und ___. 3) Ich esse gern ___./Wir essen gern ___. 4) Ich möchte ___ (trinken)./Wir möchten ___ (trinken). 5) Ja, ich habe eine Reservierung./Ja, wir haben eine Reservierung.

Culture note—Sales tax

Sales tax is already included in the price of items. This holds true not just for clothing or books or crystal, but also food in grocery stores and restaurants.

Culture note—Recycling and garbage

Germans are passionate about separating their garbage and recycling. Glass and metal go in their own bins for recycling. Garbage is separated into plastic, paper, and compost. Public trash containers frequently feature four separate bins—one for paper (*Papier*), for packaging (*Verpackung*), for glass (*Glas*), and one for everything else (*Restmüll*). Austrians also separate and recycle, but with less fervor than in Germany. Public garbage cans in Austria typically aren't separated out by type of garbage.

Useful Vocabulary

big	groß	gRohs
small	klein	kline
a lot	viel	feel
not much	wenig	vay-ni^{ch}
a little	ein bißchen	ine bis-^{ch}en
hot	heiß	hice
cold	kalt	kahlt
warm	warm	vah(r)m
good or well	gut	goot
bad	schlecht	shle^{ch}t
enough	genug	geh-nuk
not enough	nicht genug	ni^{ch}t geh-nuk
only	nur	noo(r)
also, too	auch	ow$_{ch}$

Culture note—"Hot," "warm" and "cold"

💣* Warning! Do not say *Ich bin heiß* or *Ich bin warm*, to say you are hot, or *Ich bin kalt*, to say you are cold. These constructions can have sexual meanings in German.

If you are overheated, you need to say *Mir ist warm* ("It is warm to me"), or, if you are chilled, say *Mir ist kalt* ("It is cold to me"). Or you could just say "It's hot/cold"—*Es ist heiß/kalt*.

Shopping

Virtually all travelers do some shopping, even if just for postcards. Make your shopping easier by learning some useful question and answer forms. As with food vocabulary, you'll have time to look up the word for anything specific that you want to buy, so you probably shouldn't use a lot of time memorizing lists of shopping items, unless you have the time or know it will be important.

Reality check: Shopping is one of those areas where you can get by pretty well with body language (pointing, nodding, head shaking). If you are really short on language learning time, just skim this section on shopping. You are probably best off knowing how to ask *How much?* and then being familiar with numbers so you can recognize the answer.

how much?	wieviel?	*vee-feel?*
to cost	kosten	*kos-ten*
How much does that cost?	Wieviel kostet das?	*vee-feel kos-tet dahs?*
to help	helfen	*hel-fen*
Can you help me?	Können Sie mir helfen?	*kern-en zee mee(r) hel-fen?*
Do you have ___ (here)?	Haben Sie (hier) ___?	*hah-ben zee (hee(r)) ___?*
postcards	Postkarten	*post-kah(r)-ten*
clothing	Kleider	*kly-deh(r)*
books	Bücher	*bew^ch-eh(r)*
umbrellas	Regenschirme	*Ray-gehn-shi(r)m-eh*
I would like ___.	Ich möchte ___.	*i^ch mer^ch-teh ___*
this, that	das	*dahs*
I'm looking for ___.	Ich suche ___.	*i^ch zoo-ch eh ___*
toothpaste	Zahnpasta	*tsahn-pahs-tah*
deodorant	Deodorant	*day-oh-doh-Rahnt*
writing paper	Schreibpapier	*shRipe-pah-pee(r)*
Where is ___?	Wo ist ___?	*voh ist ___?*
Where is a bookstore?	Wo ist eine Buchhandlung?	*voh ist ine-eh boo ch-hahnt-lung?*

Where are ___?	Wo sind ___?	*voh zint ___?*
Where are the shoes?	Wo sind die Schuhe?	*voh zint dee <u>shoo</u>-eh?*
to touch	berühren	*beh-<u>Rew</u>-Ren*
Don't touch!	Nicht berühren!	*ni^{ch}t beh-<u>Rew</u>-Ren*
I'm just looking.	Ich schaue nur.	*i^{ch} <u>shau</u>-eh noo(r)*
sale	Ausverkauf	*<u>ows</u>-feh(r)-kowf*
special offer	Sonderangebot	*<u>zon</u>-de(r)-ahn-geh-boht*
cash register	die Kasse	*dee <u>kahs</u>-seh*
Where do I pay?	Wo ist die Kasse?	*voh ist dee <u>kah</u>-seh?*
to take	nehmen	*<u>nay</u>-men*
I'll take it.	Ich nehme es.	*i^{ch} <u>nay</u>-meh es*
traveler's checks	Reiseschecks	*<u>Rye</u>-zeh-sheks*
Do you take traveler's checks?	Nehmen Sie Reiseschecks?	*<u>nay</u>-men zee <u>Rye</u>-zeh-sheks?*
credit cards	Kreditkarten	*kReh-<u>deet</u>-kah(r)-ten*
Do you take credit cards?	Nehmen Sie Kreditkarten?	*<u>nay</u>-men zee kReh-<u>deet</u>-kah(r)-ten?*

Culture note—das Kaufhaus

If you want to find the greatest variety of items under one roof at a reasonable price, head to a *Kaufhaus* (department store).

Stores

Where is ___?	Wo ist ___?	*voh ist ___?*
bookstore	die Buchhandlung	*dee <u>boo</u>_{ch}-hant-lung*
market	der Markt	*day(r) mah(r)kt*
supermarket	der Supermarkt	*day(r) <u>zoo</u>-peh(r)-mah(r)kt*
department store	das Kaufhaus	*dahs <u>kowf</u>-hows*
barbershop	der Friseur	*day(r) fRi-<u>zew(r)</u>*
camera store	das Fotogeschäft	*dahs <u>foh</u>-toh-geh-sheft*
bakery	die Bäckerei	*dee bek-eR-<u>eye</u>*
pastry shop	die Konditorei	*dee kon-dee-tohR-<u>eye</u>*

ice cream shop	das Eiscafé	dahs _ice_-kah-fay
	die Eisdiele	dee _ice_-dee-leh
	der Eissalon	day(r) _ice_-zah-lohn
drug store	die Drogerie	dee dRo-geh-_Ree_
pharmacy	die Apotheke	dee ah-po-_tay_-keh
entrance	der Eingang	day(r) _ine_-gahng
exit	der Ausgang	day(r) _ows_-gahng
press, push	drücken	d_Rewk_-en
pull	ziehen	_tsee_-en
opened	geöffnet	geh-_erf_-net
closed	geschlossen	geh-_shlos_-en

Culture note—Business hours

German and Austrian store hours have expanded drastically in the last decade, but opening times are still more limited than Americans are used to. Be aware that many stores are closed in the evenings, on Saturday afternoons and Sunday, and some are closed over the lunch hour, especially in smaller towns. If you are using grocery stores to limit your food expenses, make sure you stock up for Sunday on Saturday. Business hours are relaxing, however, with more stores staying open in the evenings and later on Saturday, and even on Sunday, especially in tourist areas.

Exercise 4.4
Translate the following into German.

1. Where is a bookstore?

2. I'm looking for a department store.

3. How much does that cost?

4. Excuse me. Where is a pharmacy, please?

5. I'm looking for a pastry shop.

Answers: 1) Wo ist eine Buchhandlung? 2) Ich suche ein Kaufhaus. 3) Wieviel kostet das? 4) Entschuldigung (or variation)! Wo ist eine Apotheke, bitte? 5) Ich suche eine Konditorei.

Culture note—das Lebensmittelgeschäft

The traditional German grocery store is called a *Lebensmittelgeschäft*. It is much smaller than a modern supermarket, with narrow aisles and miniature carts. Shopping in a *Lebensmittelgeschäft* (or a supermarket, for that matter) can be a high-pressure situation for unprepared Americans.

Many things are different than in the U.S. First, to those of us used to huge supermarkets with broad aisles, the smaller markets can cause a sense of claustrophobia. Also, the shopping carts may be locked together at the entrance, separable only when you deposit a coin in the appropriate slot. (You get the deposit back when you return your cart and lock it up.) The store may be crowded with shoppers, especially late afternoon and early evening, when working women rush to buy groceries on their way home.

In addition, many Americans and Brits have experienced that senior citizens are sometimes a little pushy with their carts in a grocery store. While locals swear this never happens to them, it's not uncommon for a little old lady to bump you with her cart if you are in her way. This can also occur in the line to pay for your goods, which is a stressful experience on its own.

You should know that grocery stores do not provide bags for you to put your groceries in. Local shoppers generally take baskets or linen bags when they shop and use those for carrying their goods home. If you need a bag for your purchases, you will find them for sale (plastic and fabric) at the checkout counter. If you need a bag, try to place it on top of your other items, so it will be rung up first. You need quick access to your shopping bag, because you will be expected to bag your own groceries.

This all contributes to the stress of checking out: the lines can be long and the checker will rattle off your total charges in German. It's very easy to get flustered and even to drop your money (coins

continued

rolling everywhere), especially when you realize that the cashier is already ringing up the purchases for the next customer and you have to rush to bag your own groceries.

Definitely check out a grocery store when you are abroad. It's extremely interesting to see what is similar and what is different from what you are used to. It's also a great place to grab an apple or a candy bar and some bottled water when you are out during the day. Just be prepared, so you can minimize any stress.

- Expect the store to be crowded.

- Have your money at the ready for paying.

- Be prepared to bag your own purchases.

- Be patient, and try to see the humor if a little old lady crowds you with her shopping cart.

Culture note—Bottle deposits

Savvy travelers quickly realize that popping into a grocery store or supermarket to buy bottles of water is far cheaper and more convenient than buying drinks from snack stands. Be aware that you pay a deposit on bottles (called a *Pfand*), even most plastic ones. You may not want to bother with collecting the bottles and returning them to retrieve the deposit (I don't), but instead of chucking them into the garbage, you could place them next to the wastebasket in your hotel room for the maid to redeem. That way you don't waste the deposit and the bottle gets recycled.

Clothing

clothing	die Kleider	dee <u>kly</u>-deh(r)
blouse	die Bluse	dee <u>bloo</u>-zeh
shirt—men only	das Hemd	dahs hemt
t-shirt	das T-Shirt	dahs <u>tee</u>-shi(r)t
pants	die Hose	dee <u>hoh</u>-zeh
jeans	die Jeans	dee jeenz

skirt	der Rock	*day(r) Rok*
dress	das Kleid	*dahs klite*
sweater	der Pullover	*day(r) pul-<u>oh</u>-veh(r)*
tie	die Krawatte	*dee kRah-<u>vah</u>-teh*
underwear	die Unterhose	*dee <u>oon</u>-teh(r)-hoh-zeh*
socks	die Socken	*dee <u>zok</u>-en*
hat	der Hut	*day(r) hoot*
jacket	die Jacke	*dee <u>yah</u>-keh*
shoes	die Schuhe	*dee <u>shoo</u>-eh*
handbag	die Handtasche	*dee <u>hant</u>-tah-sheh*
umbrella	der Regenschirm	*day(r) <u>Ray</u>-gehn-shi(r)m*
gloves	die Handschuhe	*dee <u>hant</u>-shoo-eh*
heavy coat	der Mantel	*day(r) <u>mahn</u>-tel*

Culture note—Clothing

Like the language and public manners, clothing in Germany and Austria is often more formal than in the United States. For example, many women still do not wear shorts in public, and if they do, their "shorts" are usually just above or, more often, below the knee. Capri pants are as short as things go for many women in the summer. They prefer slacks, skirts or dresses. And in summer they wear these items with sandals, not tennis shoes.

And for men? Some do wear shorts, although more at home than on the street, usually with sandals or dark shoes, not sport shoes. Dark socks or no socks are appropriate. Germans and Austrians don't wear white sport socks in non-sport, non-exercise situations.

Most adults do not wear athletic gear (including warm-up suits) in public unless they are going to participate in athletics (although some do choose athletic gear for their "free-time" look). Most adults don't wear tennis shoes as their daily shoes. You may certainly follow American custom on all these matters, but be aware that you will probably stand out as a tourist.

Culture note—Blue jeans

Blue jeans have evolved from being a sure sign of an American tourist to becoming the "second skin" of many Germans and Austrians. You may safely pack your jeans without fear of standing out as a tourist. As for favorite brands, Levi's are perennially popular.

Colors

black	schwarz	*shvah(r)ts*
white	weiß	*vice*
beige	beige	*bayzh*
blue	blau	*blau*
brown	braun	*bRown*
green	grün	*gRewn*
gray	grau	*gRau*
orange	orange	*oh-<u>Rahn</u>-zheh*
pink	rosa	*<u>Roh</u>-zah*
purple	violett	*vee-oh-<u>let</u>*
red	rot	*Roht*
yellow	gelb	*gelp*
silver	silbern	*<u>zil</u>-beh(r)n*
gold	golden	*<u>gol</u>-den*
light	hell	*hel*
dark	dunkel	*<u>dunk</u>-el*

You can indicate the lightness or darkness of a color by adding the word *hell* (light) or *dunkel* (dark) to the front of the color word. For example, light blue is *hellblau* and dark red is *dunkelrot*.

Culture note—Hair color

While men may gray with age in Austria, most women don't. It is extremely common for women to color their hair there. Germany shows more of a mix between color and gray.

Culture note—Nudism

Germans and Austrians may not wear shorts, but it's fine to go topless at many public swimming pools, and nude bathing at the beach is a common practice. Proponents of the family-friendly nude beaches, which are known as FKK (*Freikörperkultur* = "free body culture"), may not approve if you visit the FKK beach without taking your clothes off. Often the beaches are marked FKK, often they are screened by a hedge or something, but it can still happen that you won't know you are coming up to one until you are on it. If you end up on a nude beach, don't stare, don't approach others (especially children), and don't take pictures without permission.

Exercise 4.5
What colors are the following items?

1. the American flag
2. grass
3. coal
4. ashes
5. nectarines
6. eggplant
7. tree bark
8. the sky
9. bananas
10. wedding rings
11. peppermint ice cream

Answers: 1) rot, weiß und blau, 2) grün, 3) schwarz, 4) grau, 5) orange, 6) violett, 7) braun, 8) blau, 9) gelb, 10) golden/silbern, 11) rosa/grün

Miscellaneous Purchases

I need ___, please.	Ich brauche ___, bitte.	i^{ch} b<u>Row</u>-$_{ch}$eh ___, <u>bit</u>-eh
newspaper	die Zeitung	dee <u>tsy</u>-tung
magazine	die Zeitschrift	dee <u>tsite</u>-shRift
clock	die Uhr	dee oo(r)
watch	die Armbanduhr	dee <u>ah(r)m</u>-bahnt-oo(r)
cuckoo clock	die Kuckucksuhr	dee <u>koo</u>-kooks-oo(r)

beer stein	der Bierkrug	*day(r) bee(r)-kRuk*
battery	die Batterie	*dee bah-teh-Ree*
camera	der Fotoapparat	*day(r) foh-toh-ah-pah-Raht*
film	der Film	*day(r) film*
digital	digital	*di-gi-tahl*
memory card	die Speicherkarte	*dee shpy^{ch}-eh(r)-kah(r)-teh*
candies	die Süßigkeiten	*dee zew-si^{ch}-ky-ten*
chewing gum	der Kaugummi	*day(r) kow-gum-ee*
cigarettes	die Zigaretten	*dee tsi-gah-Ret-en*
eyeglasses	die Brille	*dee bRil-eh*
sunglasses	die Sonnenbrille	*dee zon-en-bRil-eh*
tanning oil	das Sonnenöl	*dahs zon-en-erl*
tanning lotion	die Sonnencreme	*dee zon-en-kRem*
deodorant	das Deodorant	*dahs day-oh-doh-Rahnt*
soap	die Seife	*dee zy-feh*
shampoo	das Shampoo	*dahs shahm-poo*
toothpaste	die Zahnpasta	*dee tsahn-pah-stah*
razor blade	die Rasierklinge	*dee Rah-zee(r)-kling-eh*
razor	der Rasierapparat	*day(r) Rah-zee(r)-ah-pah-Raht*
shaving cream	die Rasiercreme	*dee Rah-zee(r)-kRem*
disposable washclothes	Einweg-Waschlappen	*ine-vayk vahsh-lahp-en*
facial tissues	die Taschentücher	*dee tah-shen-tew^{ch}-eh(r)*

Exercise 4.6

Translate the following into German.

1. I need a battery, please.

2. Where are the shoes?

3. I'm looking for a blouse.

4. I would like chocolate, please.

5. I need a memory card. Here is my (mein) camera.

6. Do you have chewing gum here?

7. Where is the shampoo?

8. I need soap, please.

9. I'm looking for a jacket.

10. I would like a newspaper.

Answers: 1) Ich brauche eine Batterie, bitte. 2) Wo sind die Schuhe? 3) Ich suche eine Bluse. 4) Ich möchte Schokolade, bitte. 5) Ich brauche eine Speicherkarte. Hier ist mein Fotoapparat. 6) Haben Sie hier Kaugummi? 7) Wo ist das Shampoo? 8) Ich brauche Seife, bitte. 9) Ich suche eine Jacke. 10) Ich möchte eine Zeitung.

Culture note—Tobacconists' shops

A common sight in Germany and Austria is the tobacconist's shop (known as *die Tabakhandlung* in Germany and *die Tabaktrafik* in Austria). The tobacconist carries much more than tobacco goods, however. Here you might also find stamps, postcards, magazines, newspapers, bus or streetcar tickets and more.

Useful Vocabulary

open	geöffnet	*geh-erf-net*
closed	geschlossen	*geh-shlos-en*
early	früh	*fRew*
late	spät	*shpate*
more	mehr	*may(r)*
less	weniger	*vay-ni^{ch}-eh(r)*
expensive	teuer	*toy-eh(r)*
cheap	billig	*bil-i^{ch}*
a good buy	günstig	*gewn-sti^{ch}*
nearby	in der Nähe	*in day(r) nay-eh*
far	weit	*vite*
up	auf	*owf*
down	unten	*un-ten*

Exercise 4.7
Match the following items with where you could buy them.

1.	_____ Buch	A.	Apotheke
2.	_____ Zeitung	B.	Bäckerei
3.	_____ Shampoo	C.	Tabakhandlung
4.	_____ Speicherkarte	D.	Drogerie
5.	_____ Torte	E.	Buchhandlung
6.	_____ Aspirin	F.	Konditorei
7.	_____ Brot	G.	Fotogeschäft

Answers: 1) E, 2) C, 3) D, 4) G, 5) F, 6) A, 7) B

Reality check: You could actually buy the above items at several different kinds of stores. This exercise was unrealistically picky!

Grammar—Past tense *sein* and *haben*

subject	to be	to have
ich	war	hatte
Sie	waren	hatten
wir	waren	hatten

Often when talking in a foreign language, you want to refer to something that took place in the past. We're not going to go over the past tense in any detail, but it's pretty easy to learn a couple of the most useful forms—"was"/"were" and "had."

The German word for "was" is *war (vah(r))*. To say, "I was," you would say in German *ich war*. "You were" or "We were" uses the form *waren* (again, the -en ending): *Sie waren* (or *Waren Sie?*) and *Wir waren*. "We were in Munich yesterday" is expressed as *Wir waren gestern in München*.

The past tense for "to have" is based on *hatten*. "I had" is *ich hatte*, "you had" is *Sie hatten*, and "we had" is *wir hatten*. "We had reservations," for example, is *Wir hatten Reservierungen*.

Culture note—Eis

A great break from sightseeing is a visit to an ice cream parlor (*Eisdiele, Eiscafe* or *Eissalon*). My family loves the variety of ice cream available across Germany and Austria, and we typically indulge in it at least once a day when we're touring. Probably our favorite flavor is the tart, zesty *Zitrone* (lemon), which combines very well with *Himbeere* (raspberry), *Orange*, or *Erdbeere* (strawberry), if you are looking for a pair of flavors to try out.

You may buy ice cream cones from vendors on the street, but fancier ice-cream concoctions should be eaten in an *Eissalon*. If you just want a cone, you order and pay at the counter. (You can still sit, though.) If you order something larger, you will order, receive the bill, pay and tip at the table.

You order a cone of ice cream (*eine Eistüte*) or bowls of mixed ice cream (*gemischtes*) by the scoop (*Kugel*). Technically, a *Kugel* is a sphere, implying a round shape, but usually the ice cream is just smashed in layers, one on top of the other, or in vaguely ball-shaped forms.

You might see a container of wafers or waffle cookies in the middle of the table. You may take as many as you want, but they are not free. Tell the waiter how many you had when you request the bill. If your ice cream treat comes *with* wafers and cookies, those are already included in the price.

Whipped cream often costs extra at an *Eissalon*, and is called *Schlagsahne* or *Schlagobers* (*schlag* means "beaten" or "whipped," *Sahne* means "cream," and *Obers* means "topping"). The first term is used mostly in Germany, and the second one mostly in Austria. Both can be shortened to *Schlag*. Practice saying it—"*Mit Schlag, bitte.*" Now say it again. OK, not everyone likes whipped cream or thinks it's worth the extra price, but it's well worth the cost, in my book, and if I'm on vacation, I'm going to enjoy every bite of it.

Grammar—Accusative case

Any German language book eventually needs to discuss what are called grammatical "cases." So far, almost everything we've talked about has been in the *nominative* case, which leaves nouns in their basic, unchanged state. The subject (the "do-er") of a sentence is in the nominative case. So are nouns that follow certain verbs. These "nominative" verbs function basically as an equal sign, as in the sentences *Ich heiße Frau Braun (ich = Frau Braun)* and *Das ist die Tür (das = Tür).* There's no sort of "action" or "influence" going on. One side of the verb is "equal" to the other side. We're just identifying, or *naming,* as the term *nominative* implies.

It doesn't take long before you want to do more with the language than just name things, though. That takes us to verbs that involve a "non-equal" relationship between things or people, often a kind of "action." Much of this action is through verbs that trigger the accusative case. The most common accusative verb is *to have* (or *haben,* in German). Nouns affected by an accusative verb are in the accusative case. That means they might have to change their form a little to be grammatically correct. Consider the difference in English between *he* and *him. He* is in the nominative case; *him* is in the accusative case. If we hear *I see he* in English, we know what the speaker means, but we also know that it isn't "right." It's the same way in German. You don't have to learn anything about the accusative case to communicate effectively, but your speech will sound better if you do.

So what's different in the accusative case than in the nominative case? Fortunately, only masculine nouns are affected. The definite and indefinite articles change from *der* and *ein* to *den* and *einen.* (See the table below.) Notice the difference in the nominative and accusative verbs. *That is the table* depicts an "equal" relationship: *that = table.* Therefore, *table* is in the nominative case. *I see the table,* on the other hand, involves a non-equal relationship: *I is not = table.* Thus, *table,* being acted on by the verb, is in the accusative case. It is called the direct object of the verb. When *table* is in the accusative case, *der Tisch* changes to *den Tisch (Ich sehe den Tisch),* and *ein Tisch* changes to *einen Tisch (Ich sehe einen Tisch).*

Reality check: Remember, knowing German grammar is just the icing on your communication cake. You *do not* need to know the accusative case to communicate quite well in German. It just sounds better. If you don't want to worry about the extra accuracy, then don't. Skip this section.

Masc. Articles	Nominative Case	Accusative Case
definite article: the	der Das ist der Tisch. *That is the table.*	den Ich sehe den Tisch. *I see the table.*
indefinite article: a/an	ein Das ist ein Tisch. *That is a table.*	einen Ich sehe einen Tisch. *I see a table.*

Some nominative verbs: sein (to be), heißen (to be called), werden (to become)

Some accusative verbs: haben (to have), sehen (to see), kaufen (to buy), empfehlen (to recommend), möchten (would like), nehmen (to take), brauchen (to need), suchen (to look for)

Remember: Only the form of masculine articles is affected. (Well, and some masculine nouns, but we won't get into that.) Feminine, neuter and plural articles stay the same in the accusative case.

Exercise 4.8
Identify whether the italicized word is in the nominative or accusative case.

1.   Das ist *das Fenster*.

2.   Ich heiße *Müller*.

3. Ich habe *einen Kuli.*

4. *Das Zimmer* ist sehr schön.

5. Wir nehmen *das Zimmer.*

6. Hier ist *mein Mann.*

7. Ich sehe *meinen Mann.*

8. Das ist *eine Jacke.*

9. Ich habe *eine Jacke.*

10. Ich brauche *Zigaretten,* bitte.

11. Wir möchten *zwei Bier.*

12. Können Sie *einen Wein* empfehlen?

13. Suchen Sie *etwas?*

14. Wo ist *das Restaurant?*

15. Möchten Sie *einen Regenschirm?*

Anwers: 1) nom., 2) nom., 3) acc., 4) nom., 5) acc., 6) nom., 7) acc., 8) nom., 9) acc., 10) acc., 11) acc., 12) acc., 13) acc., 14) nom., 15) acc.

Culture note—Crossing the street

When you cross the street, you need to wait at the corner for the green pedestrian light to show. If the traffic light has changed to green but the pedestrian light is still red, look for a button on the light post to push, to signal that you want the light to change. You will probably need to wait for the next cycle to get a green signal.

If the "cross" light is already on when you get to the intersection, you may cross the street. If the "cross" light is flashing, however, that means it will soon change back to red. If you are already in the street when the light changes to red, you are allowed to finish crossing. Keep an eye out for bad drivers, though, even if you are in a pedestrian zone.

Cuture note—Public drinking fountains

Don't expect to find public drinking fountains in Germany and Austria. On a recent three-week tourist trip through both countries, I saw a grand total of *one* public drinking fountain. Try to get in the practice of taking a bottle of water with you when you are out for the day.

Grammar—Question word order

You know from Chapter One that word order changes in questions. Still, you can identify who or what is doing the action (the *subject*) and who or what is "receiving" the action (the *direct object*). For example, in the question *Was möchten Sie essen?* (What would you like to eat?), the subject (who will do the eating) is *Sie*, and the direct object (what will be eaten) is *was*, which is the first word. The direct object is in the accusative case, even if it's not where you expect it to be in the sentence.

Exercise 4.9

How would you say the following in German?

1. I have the book.

2. I'm looking for a bakery.

3. I would like a coffee, please.

4. Do you have enough money?

5. Can you recommend a hotel?

6. We will take the bus (*der Bus*).

7. Do you take credit cards?

8. I would like a beer.

9. Do we need an umbrella?

10. Do you speak English?

Answers: 1) Ich habe das Buch. 2) Ich suche eine Bäckerei. 3) Ich möchte einen Kaffee, bitte. 4) Haben Sie genug Geld? 5) Können Sie ein Hotel empfehlen? 6) Wir nehmen den Bus. 7) Nehmen Sie Kreditkarten? 8) Ich möchte ein Bier. 9) Brauchen wir einen Regenschirm? 10) Sprechen Sie English?

Culture note—die Garderobe

You may want to check your coat and bags at some tourist sights, or you may have to, even if you don't want to. Look for the room or counter labeled *Garderobe* (checkroom). You may be charged or expected to tip for this service.

Culture note—Tipping and donations

If you have a guided tour of a sight, you might slip your guide a small tip at the end of the tour. (This custom is changing, though.) Also, while most churches are open for free viewing, church authorities do appreciate (and sometimes expect) a contribution to the donation box, usually located near the entrance.

Culture note—Cobblestone streets

Many old European streets and sidewalks are paved with cobble-stones, which are picturesque and romantic but can be rough on the feet. Cobblestones can range from flat stones to highly round-ed ones. The stones (especially the round ones) can get very slick when wet. If you will be walking a lot, wear thick-soled, sturdy shoes.

Culture note—Bicycle paths

Bicycles are used much more as a means of transportation in Europe than in the U.S. Many German and Austrian cities have official bicycle paths, usually a narrow lane between the sidewalk and the street. Avoid walking on the bike paths. If you suddenly hear a bell shrilling behind you (it's always startling), you are probably on the bike path and a cyclist wants to get around you.

It's not always the pedestrian who is at fault, though, in encount-ers with bicyclists. Be aware that some cyclists do not follow the rules for where they are *not* supposed to ride, and some do not yield the right-of-way when they are supposed to. Be ever alert to bicyclists, even in areas where they are not supposed to ride their bikes, if you want to avoid potential collisions. Yes, cyclists are often breaking the rules, but you are still the one to get bumped and bruised, if you don't watch out.

Sightseeing

Seeing the sights is a major part of most trips abroad. Learn some basic vocabulary to find your way more easily.

Where is ___?	Wo ist ___?	*voh ist ___?*
the cathedral	der Dom	*day(r) dohm*
the church	die Kirche	*day(r) ki(r)-ᶜʰeh*
the old town	die Altstadt	*dee ahlt-shtaht*
the main square	der Hauptplatz	*day(r) howpt-plahts*
the market square	der Marktplatz	*day(r) mah(r)kt-plahts*
the town hall	das Rathaus	*dahs Raht-hows*
the museum	das Museum	*dahs mu-zay-um*
the fortress	die Festung	*dee fest-ung*
the palace	das Schloß	*dahs shlos*
	der Palast	*day(r) pah-lahst*
the castle	die Burg	*dee booRk*
	das Schloß	*dahs shlos*
the house	das Haus	*dahs hows*
the building	das Gebäude	*dahs geh-boy-deh*
the park	der Park	*day(r) pah(r)k*
the garden	der Garten	*day(r) gah(r)-ten*
the bridge	die Brücke	*dee bRew-keh*
the fountain	der Brunnen	*day(r) bRu-nen*
tourist information	die Touristen-information	*dee too-Ris-ten-in-fo(r)-mah-tsyohn*
a sightseeing tour	eine Stadtrundfahrt	*ine-eh shtaht-Runt-fah(r)t*
city map	der Stadtplan	*day(r) shtaht-plahn*
entrance	der Eingang	*day(r) ine-gahng*
exit	der Ausgang	*day(r) ows-gahng*
entrance ticket	die Eintrittskarte	*dee ine-tRits-kah(r)-teh*
adults	Erwachsene	*eh(r)-vahᶜʰ-seh-neh*
forbidden	verboten	*feh(r)-boh-ten*
No photography allowed!	Fotographieren verboten!	*foh-toh-gRah-feeR-en feh(r)-boht-en*
No smoking!	Rauchen verboten!	*Rau-ᶜʰen feh(r)-boh-ten*

Exercise 4.10

Translate into German.

1. Where is the entrance?

2. We need a city map, please.

3. I need an entrance ticket.

4. How much does an entrance ticket cost, please?

5. Where is the cathedral?

6. I'm looking for the old town.

7. Go straight ahead and then left.

8. I see the park.

9. I would like to buy two entrance tickets.

10. Two adults.

11. Where is Information?

12. There is the castle.

13. Where is the town hall?

14. Go right until the (*bis zur*) church.

Answers: 1) Wo ist der Eingang? 2) Wir brauchen einen Stadtplan, bitte. 3) Ich brauche eine Eintrittskarte. 4) Wieviel kostet eine Eintrittskarte, bitte? 5) Wo ist der Dom? 6) Ich suche die Altstadt. 7) Gehen Sie geradeaus und dann links. 8) Ich sehe den Park. 9) Ich möchte zwei Eintrittskarten kaufen. 10) Zwei Erwachsene. 11) Wo ist die Auskunft/die Touristeninformation? 12) Da ist die Burg/das Schloß. 13) Wo ist das Rathaus? 14) Gehen Sie rechts bis zur Kirche.

Culture note—City bus tours

Commercial city bus tours can be a comfortable and convenient way to get a city overview. If you are sick and tired of hoofing it, or the weather is awful, it might be well worth the money to sit on a climate-controlled bus for a couple of hours. Many cities have tour buses that allow you to get on and off at major sights, which can be more convenient than taking public transportation.

5   Services, Arrival and Transportation

Numbers (21-99)

Once you learn how to count in the twenties, thirties, etc., up to 100, you will have the hardest part of the number system behind you. Review the numbers you already know before you attack the new ones: count from 0 to 20, then from 0 to 100 by tens. Then look at the new numbers below. (I've added hyphens to the words to make them easier to read.)

20	zwanzig	*tsvahn-tsi^{ch}*
21	ein-und-zwanzig	*ine-unt-tsvahn-tsi^{ch}*
22	zwei-und-zwanzig	*tsvy-unt-tsvahn-tsi^{ch}*
23	drei-und-zwanzig	*dRy-unt-tsvahn-tsi^{ch}*
24	vier-und-zwanzig	*fee(r)-unt-tsvahn-tsi^{ch}*
25	fünf-und-zwanzig	*fewnf-unt-tsvahn-tsi^{ch}*
26	sechs-und-zwanzig	*ze^{ch}s-unt-tsvahn-tsi^{ch}*
27	sieben-und-zwanzig	*zee-ben-unt-tsvahn-tsi^{ch}*
28	acht-und-zwanzig	*ah$_{ch}$t-unt-tsvahn-tsi^{ch}*
29	neun-und-zwanzig	*noyn-unt-tsvahn-tsi^{ch}*
30	dreißig	*dRy-si^{ch}*
31	ein-und-dreißig	*ine-unt-dRy-si^{ch}*
42	zwei-und-vierzig	*tsvy-unt-fee(r)-tsi^{ch}*
53	drei-und-fünfzig	*dRy-unt-fewnf-tsi^{ch}*
64	vier-und-sechzig	*fee(r)-unt-ze^{ch}-tsi^{ch}*
75	fünf-und-siebzig	*fewnf-unt-zeep-tsi^{ch}*
86	sechs-und-achtzig	*ze^{ch}s-unt-ah$_{ch}$-tsi^{ch}*
97	sieben-und-neunzig	*zee-ben-unt-noyn-tsi^{ch}*
98	acht-und-neunzig	*ah$_{ch}$t-unt-noyn-tsi^{ch}*
99	neun-und-neunzig	*noyn-unt-noyn-tsi^{ch}*

As you can see, the German system for forming numbers 21 through 99 is different from the English system. It *is* like the

English system for numbers 13 through 19, though. In the English teens, we put the small part of the number (*four*) in front of the big part of the number (*teen*). German follows this pattern up through 99. So, 23 is *drei-und-zwanzig*, 24 is *vier-und-zwanzig*, etc. While this system feels very foreign to us, you can find it in some old forms of English, such as *four and twenty blackbirds*.

Using the table below as a guide, count from 21-99. Combine the numbers of the left column with the number 20 to get 21-29, then go through all combinations with the number 30, and so on, until you reach 100. Run through all the numbers a couple of times, until they start to feel a little more natural.

Forming numbers 21-99

1		20
2		30
3		40
4		50
5	*und*	60
6		70
7		80
8		90
9		

Exercise 5.1
Can you read the following numbers out loud?

1. 93

2. 61

3. 27

4. 88

5. 49

6. 72

7. 56

8. 65

9. 34

10. 41

Answers: 1) drei-und-neunzig, 2) ein-und-sechzig, 3) sieben-und-zwanzig, 4) acht-und-achtzig, 5) neun-und-vierzig, 6) zwei-und-siebzig, 7) sechs-und-fünfzig, 8) fünf-und-sechzig, 9) vier-und-dreißig, 10) ein-und-vierzig (Correctly written, the German numbers are each one long word, without hyphens.)

Telling Time

Telling time in a foreign language always seems confusing, at least at first. You might want to familiarize yourself with ways of asking and telling time.

The most common way to ask the time is:

Wie spät ist es?   How late is it? = What time is it?

There are two common ways of telling the time. The first one (A) is with the minute reading mentioned before the hour reading (It's ten after four) (*Es ist zehn nach vier*). I think of this as "analog" time, the way people say the time when they are looking at a traditional clock face.

The other way (B), involves reading the hour before the minute (It's four ten), separated by the word *Uhr* (o'clock) (*Es ist vier Uhr zehn*). This is "digital" time to me, because it's how people read a digital display of time, from left to right.

Reality check: As a tourist, you will usually care only about opening and closing times, which you will be able to read either on signs or in your guidebook. Save yourself some trouble. Unless you will be setting or keeping appointments, just take a watch along and don't worry about telling time in German.

A. Es ist _____ (Uhr).

Es ist <u>eins</u>.	or	Es ist <u>ein Uhr</u>.
Es ist <u>zwei</u>.	or	Es ist <u>zwei Uhr</u>.
Es ist <u>drei</u>.	or	Es ist <u>drei Uhr</u>.

This pattern continues through twelve (*zwölf*) or twenty-four (*vierundzwanzig*), if you are using the twenty-four-hour clock. Note that the word for *one* changes very slightly, depending on whether you include the word *Uhr* in your answer. This is an exception to the regular pattern.

In English, when it is thirty minutes past the hour, we say that it is *half past* the hour. In German, you look ahead to the next hour and say that it is halfway *to* that hour. (Note, Germans use a period instead of a colon when they write times.)

2.30 = halb drei
9.30 = halb zehn

The word for *after* is *nach*. The word for *before* or *to* is *vor*.

3.12 = zwölf nach drei
11.23 = dreiundzwanzig nach elf

12.52 = acht vor eins
4.55 = fünf vor fünf

The word for *quarter* is *Viertel*.

1.15 = Viertel nach eins
9.45 = Viertel vor zehn

The word for *midnight* is *Mitternacht*. The word for *noon* is *Mittag*.

B.   Many people find the second way of saying the time easier:

Es ist _____ Uhr _____.

6.20 = Es ist sechs Uhr zwanzig.
7.43 = Es ist sieben Uhr dreiundvierzig.

Culture note—24-hour clock

Europeans use the 24-hour clock (also known as military time) for official designations of time (for example, on train, bus, or TV schedules) and often in casual usage. If you see a time listed as 20.00, just remember to subtract twelve to get the "real" time, eight p.m. In casual speech, German speakers do not always use the 24-hour clock. They differentiate between a.m and p.m. by saying *morgens* for morning times and *abends* for evening times. For example, *acht Uhr morgens* means 8:00 a.m., while *acht Uhr abends* means 8:00 p.m.

Exercise 5.2

How do you say the following times in German?

1. quarter after one
2. six twenty-three
3. twelve to seven
4. four-thirty
5. eleven twenty-five
6. quarter to two
7. ten-thirty
8. midnight
9. noon

Answers: 1) Viertel nach eins/Viertel nach ein Uhr, 2) sechs Uhr dreiundzwanzig, 3) zwölf vor sieben (Uhr), 4) halb fünf, 5) elf Uhr fünfundzwanzig/fünf vor halb zwölf, 6) Viertel vor zwei (Uhr), 7) halb elf, 8) Mitternacht, 9) Mittag

---

Culture note—Pedestrian rules

When out in public, Germans and Austrians usually follow these pedestrian rules. They will appreciate it if you do, too.

1. Wait for the light at intersections.
2. Don't jaywalk.
3. Don't litter.

Bathrooms

Let's not overlook the obvious. Some vital vocabulary. . . .

bathroom, toilet	die Toilette	*dee toy-<u>let</u>-teh*
bathroom, water closet	das WC	*dahs vay-<u>tsay</u>*
ladies	die Damen	*dee <u>dah</u>-men*
gentlemen	die Herren	*dee <u>hay</u>R-en*
toilet paper	das Toilettenpapier	*dahs toy-<u>let</u>-ten-pah-pee(r)*
paper towels	Papiertücher	*pah-<u>pee(r)</u>-tew^{ch}-eh(r)*

Culture note—Bathroom fees, toilets and etiquette

You frequently need to pay a small fee to use a public toilet in Germany or Austria. Often the bathroom stall door will have a coin lock, typically requiring a 50-cent piece. (You may want to save some of these coins for that purpose.) If the bathroom is instead served by an attendant who keeps it clean, on your way out you should drop a tip in the small dish that will be sitting out in the bathroom or right outside it. Do leave a tip. It's bad manners not to tip the attendant, and some of them get angry when there's no tip. More than one naïve tourist has been chased from a bathroom by an irrate attendant, never knowing what went wrong.

Men, be prepared to find female attendants in the men's room, and women, be prepared to find men. Try not to feel too uncomfortable. They're used to working in there and won't be embarrassed. You shouldn't be, either.

German and Austrian toilets are often different in design than American ones. Instead of containing a big bowl of water, some really old models have a kind of shelf inside, which is swept clean by water when you flush. Next to virtually every toilet you will find a small toilet brush, to be used for cleaning up the bowl or shelf after you have used the toilet.

European toilets also have different flushing mechanisms than American ones do. If you don't see a familiar lever to press, look for a pull-knob or a push-button on the top (or possibly the side) of the toilet. The flushing lever may be on the wall above the back of the toilet. If the toilet tank is located high above the toilet, it may have a chain for you to pull in order to flush. Many toilets have two levers for flushing, a smaller one and a larger one. The smaller one releases less water and is for "small jobs," and the larger lever is used when more water is needed. This is one of many ways Germans and Austrians conserve resources.

Public toilets can be marked in numerous ways: *Toiletten, WC, 00,* or, rarely, *Abort.*

Culture note—Bathroom privacy

When you use the bathroom, even in a private home, you are expected to lock the door, otherwise people won't know the bathroom is in use and you could be walked in on, embarrassing both parties.

Many Americans are pleasantly surprised to find that public bathrooms in Germany and Austria often have stall walls and doors that run from floor to ceiling, providing welcome privacy.

Culture note—Toilet paper

German and Austrian toilet paper has come a long way from its "construction paper" days, but much of it is still mighty stiff and rough. I suspect it's because of environmental concerns—either it's made of recycled paper, or it biodegrades more easily, or both. Despite its stiffness, you will be plenty happy to find some at a public toilet, at least at those that don't have an attendant on duty to keep the stalls stocked. There are even public toilets now where there is no fee for the toilet, but you have to buy toilet paper from an automat. Check for that if you enter a "no-cost" toilet. As a precaution, it's best to keep a little extra toilet paper from your hotel with you when you go out, just in case.

Exchanging Money

money	das Geld	*dahs gelt*
to exchange	wechseln	*ve^ch-seln*
currency exchange office	die Wechselstube	*dee ve^ch-sel-shtoo-beh*
I would like to exchange money.	Ich möchte Geld wechseln.	*i^ch mer^ch-teh gelt ve^ch-seln*
I would like euros, please.	Ich möchte Euro, bitte.	*i^ch mer^ch-teh oy-Roh, bit-eh*
automatic teller machine	der Geldautomat	*day(r) gelt-ow-toh-maht*
	der Bankomat	*day(r) bahnk-oh-maht*
exchange rate	der Kurs	*day(r) ku(r)z*

Culture note—ATMs and exchanging money

With the rapid spread of ATMs, exchanging money has become obsolete. It's easier and cheaper to get money from an ATM than to exchange it. If your cash or debit card has a Plus or Cirrus logo, just look for an ATM (*Geldautomat*, marked with a blue "e"/red "c" symbol, or in Austria a *Bankomat*, usually marked with a green/blue "B") that shows Plus or Cirrus affiliation.

You can even find exact locations of compatible machines before you go by checking with your bank or looking the information up on the Internet. To use the Web, go to *www.mastercard.com* for Cirrus listings and *www.visa.com* for Plus listings. On the opening page, choose the United States as your location, then, when the U.S. page comes up, click on the link to the ATM locator.

At the time of this writing, German ATMs did not give the choice of withdrawing money from a checking account or a savings account—checking was the only option. If, like my brother-in-law, you intend to withdraw from a savings account, you could come up empty-handed at the cash machine, *not* the situation you want to be in if you are relying on the ATM to pay for your trip. In my brother-in-law's case, he had to phone his home bank from Germany to clear up the problem, and *they* had to create a temporary checking account for him, so he could access the money in his savings account.

When getting cash from an ATM, you might choose to select an "odd" number for your withdrawal, rather than a "round" number, like 100 euros. If the machine gives you a 100 euro bill for a 100 euro withdrawal (as has happened to me), you could have a terrible time trying to break that bill. A request for 95 euros (if allowed) would guarantee a much more useful selection of bills.

Should you choose not to use ATMs to get cash, you can exchange money at banks (called either *die Bank* or *die Sparkasse*), at many post offices, or at exchange booths in airports or train stations. Be aware that you pay a fee each time you exchange money, and the fees are higher at airports and train stations.

Mail and E-Mail Service

post office	die Post	*dee post*
mail	die Post	*dee post*
letter	der Brief	*day(r) bReef*
postcard	die Postkarte	*dee post-kah(r)-teh*
stamp	die Briefmarke	*dee bReef-mah(r)-keh*
to America	nach Amerika	*nah_{ch} ah-meh-Ri-kah*
by airmail	per Luftpost	*peh(r) luft-post*
I need stamps to America.	Ich brauche Briefmarken nach Amerika.	*i^{ch} brow-_{ch}eh bReef-mah(r)-ken na_{ch} ah-meh-Ri-kah*
mailbox	der Briefkasten	*day(r) bReef-kah-sten*
e-mail	die E-Mail	*dee ee-mayl*
to read	lesen	*lay-zen*
to send	schicken	*shik-en*

Culture note—E-mail and Internet use

E-mail and the Internet are just as popular in Germany and Austria as in the United States. Some hotels have computers available for Internet use either free or for a charge. *Internet Cafés* are popular venues for checking e-mail or surfing the Net. You pay a fee to use a computer for a certain length of time.

The German keyboard has keys that an American one doesn't (all those umlauted letters. . .), but the biggest challenge is that the Z and Y keys are reversed. The second challenge is that you have to reach farther to the sides to get the shift keys. The @-symbol needed for e-mail addresses is on the Q key—hit it along with the key just to the right of the space bar (labeled "Alt Gr"). Be aware that hypens and apostrophes are also in different locations. The keyboard challenges aren't insurmountable, of course, but they will slow down your typing.

A current travel guide book should list locations of *Internet Cafés* in the town you are in. You could also ask at the tourist information office or at the desk of your hotel.

Culture note—die Post

Yellow-gold is the official color of the postal service. The post office will bear a yellow-gold sign, and mail boxes and slots will be the same color.

Exercise 5.3

What would you say in the following situations?

1. You're looking for a bathroom.

2. You're looking for an Internet Café.

3. You need euros.

4. You're looking for a post office.

5. You need stamps to America.

Answers: 1) Wo ist die Toilette, bitte?/Ich suche eine Toilette. 2) Wo ist ein Internet Café, bitte?/Ich suche ein Internet Café. 3) Ich brauche Euro, bitte. 4) Wo ist die Post, bitte?/Ich suche die Post. 5) Ich brauche Briefmarken nach Amerika, bitte.

Arrival

Your arrival in Germany or Austria will be less confusing if you know what some of the words around you mean. You should be able to recognize these terms when you see them, but you shouldn't need to produce them yourself, unless you want to ask where the information desk or the luggage carousel is.

passport control	die Kontrolle	*dee kon-tRol-eh*
passport	der (Reise)Paß	*day(r) (Ry-zeh)-pahs*
Your passport, please.	Ihren Paß, bitte.	*eeR-en pahs, bit-eh*
customs	der Zoll	*day(r) tsol*
identification	der Ausweis	*day(r) ows-vice*
Do you speak English?	Sprechen Sie Englisch?	*shpReh^ch-en zee eng-lish?*
Can you help me?	Können Sie mir helfen?	*kern-en zee mee(r) hel-fen?*

information	die Auskunft	*dee ows-kunft*
luggage	das Gepäck	*dahs geh-pek*
airport	der Flughafen	*day(r) fluk-hah-fen*
flight	der Flug	*day(r) fluk*

The Alphabet

You sometimes need to spell words as a traveler, such as your name. Also, announcements in airports and train stations may include letters identifying boarding gates or platform locations.

In addition, you need to know how to pronounce letters if you want to properly be able to say abbreviations such as the following: WC (bathroom), VW (car), BMW (car), A1 (Autobahn number), B42 (highway number), FKK (nude beach designation), PKW ("passenger car"), LKW ("truck"), or USA.

Consequently, while it's not necessary to be able to say the alphabet forward and backward in German, it's not a bad idea to familiarize yourself with it a little bit.

a	*ah*	**p**	*pay*
b	*bay*	**q**	*koo*
c	*tsay*	**r**	*ay(r)*
d	*day*	**s**	*es*
e	*ay*	**t**	*tay*
f	*eff*	**u**	*oo*
g	*gay*	**v**	*fow*
h	*hah*	**w**	*vay*
i	*ee*	**x**	*iks*
j	*yott*	**y**	*ewp-sil-on*
k	*kah*	**z**	*tset*
l	*ell*	**ß**	*es-tset/shah(r)-fes es*
m	*emm*	**ä**	*ah-oom-lowt*
n	*enn*	**ö**	*oh-oom-lowt*
o	*oh*	**ü**	*oo-oom-lowt*

Exercise 5.4

What German words do the following series of letters spell?
Letters are indicated by their pronunciations.

1. yott / ah

2. gay / ay / ell / day

3. ah / bay / ay/ enn / day

4. es / pay / ah-oom-lowt / tay

5. hah / ay / ee / es-tset

6. tset / ee / emm / emm / ay / ay(r)

7. es / tsay / hah / ell / oh / es-tset

8. pay / eff / ell / ah / oo / emm / ay

9. emm / ah-oom-lowt / ay(r) / tset

10. ell / ah / enn / gay / es / ah / emm

11. fow / ay / ay(r) / es / tay / ay / hah / ay

12. tay / es / tsay / hah / oo-oom-lowt / es

13. vay / oh / tsay / hah / ay / enn / ay / enn / day / ay

14. eff / ay(r) / oo-oom-lowt / hah / es / tay / oo-oom-lowt / tsay / kah

15. ay(r) / oh / tay / vay / ay / ee / enn

16. pay / ah / pay / ee / ay / ay(r) / kah / oh / ay(r) / bay

17. fow / ay / ay(r) / tset / ay / ee / hah / oo / enn / gay

18. kah / ah / ah(r) / tay / oh / eff / eff / ay / ell

19. oh-oom-lowt / ess / tay / ay / ay(r) / ay(r) / ay / ee / tsay / hah

Answers: 1) ja, 2) Geld, 3) Abend, 4) spät, 5) heiß, 6) Zimmer, 7) Schloß,
8) Pflaume, 9) März, 10) langsam, 11) verstehe, 12) tschüs, 13) Wochenende,
14) Frühstück, 15) Rotwein, 16) Papierkorb, 17) Verzeihung, 18) Kartoffel,
19) Österreich

Travel tip: The day from hell

Warning: The first day in Europe is usually pretty bad. Always the worst day of the trip, for me. Don't get discouraged if the start of your longed-for, dreamed-about trip is a huge disappointment. You have to get through customs, through the airport, and find money, transportation and your hotel, all in a different language, a different culture, and in less-than-your-finest form after little or no sleep on the plane.

I strongly advise travelers to keep their first day simple. Reserve lodging fairly close to your arrival airport, and check in early, so you don't have to worry about finding your hotel when you're even more tired and feeling the pressure of evening coming on.

Transportation

Unless you are with a tour group with all transportation provided, you should be familiar with the most important means of getting around.

taxi	das Taxi	dahs _tahk_-see
to ___	zu ___	tsoo ___
Please stop here.	Bitte, halten Sie hier!	_bit_-eh, _hahl_-ten zee hee(r)
ticket	die Fahrkarte	dee _fah(r)_-kah(r)-teh
bus	der Bus	day(r) bus
subway	die U-Bahn	dee _oo_-bahn
streetcar	die Straßenbahn	dee _shtRah_-sen-bahn
city & suburban train	die S-Bahn	dee _es_-bahn
train	der Zug	day(r) tsook
train station	der Bahnhof	day(r) _bahn_-hof
main train station	der Hauptbahnhof	day(r) _howpt_-bahn-hof
boat	das Boot	dahs boht
to rent	mieten	_mee_-ten
bicycle	das Fahrrad	dahs _fah(r)_-Rahd
motorcycle	das Motorrad	dahs moh-_to(r)_-Rahd

Culture note—Ticket checks

Always make sure you have a valid ticket to ride public transportation. You usually need to validate your own ticket on subways, buses and streetcars. Look for a little box to stick your ticket into (either at the stop or on the vehicle itself) so your ticket will be stamped with the date and time.

Tickets are checked during train trips and may be checked at any time on other forms of transportation. You may need to show your ticket when exiting public transportation, at the subway exit, for example, so hold on to your ticket, even if you are done riding for the moment. If you are caught riding without a valid ticket, you could face a hefty fine. Yes, tourists, too.

Culture note—Buses

Some city buses are double deckers. You climb a mini spiral staircase to reach the upper level, where you can have a better vantage point for viewing the city. Just make sure you give yourself plenty of time to descend and leave the bus at your stop. Be aware that buses aren't air conditioned, and the great view at the front of the upper level comes at the cost of no air flow.

Bus stops are marked with a large H, for *Haltestelle* ("stopping spot").

Culture note—Preferential seating

Seats near the doors of streetcars, buses and subways are supposed to be made available for people of lesser physical capacities. If the vehicle is full, you are expected to give up those marked seats for the old, infirm, blind, pregnant, and those with babies. Kind, well-mannered, able-bodied riders will offer their seats to others who need them, even if they are not in a specially marked one. This is an opportunity to make a good impression and give yourself a warm feeling, knowing you have done a good deed.

Culture note—Es zieht!

Many Germans and Austrians, especially older ones, *loathe* drafts. This extends to cars and buses, where windows might be shut tight even on the hottest days.

This aversion almost drove my breeze-loving mother crazy one summer when she was living in Germany. She was the first person on the local bus she rode daily to Regensburg, and she would open all the windows to catch the summer breezes. As older women boarded the bus at later stops, they would invariably cry, *"Es zieht! Es zieht!"* ("It's drafty!") and close all the windows on the bus.

This was a daily battle that my mother never won, and she is hardly alone—it happens all the time. Germans and Austrians love fresh air and will fling open their bedroom windows on a cold winter day to air their bedding on the window sill, but drafts are generally considered uncomfortable and even dangerous. (Air conditioning is also commonly regarded as dangerous to one's health.) When traveling or visiting, don't expect to see ceiling fans or other fans or anything designed to circulate air. It's just not done. And good luck keeping your bus window open. Even if no one closes it for you (and they just might), you are likely to hear complaints of *"Es zieht!"* from people sitting behind you, pressuring you to close the window yourself.

Travel tip: Make sure you have a decent map (*eine Landkarte*). You should get a basic map with your rental car, but you may want to bring a good one with you, if you plan to drive a lot.

Travel tip: Check your auto insurance policy and your credit cards to see whether they include international auto insurance in their coverage. Mine cover everything except personal liability, and my umbrella policy at home covers that, so I am able to decline the pricey car insurance. In fact, if I want my credit card's insurance to cover any collision costs, then I am *required* to sign the rental company's collision waiver.

Renting a Car

Virtually anyone you would rent a car from is used to dealing with tourists and will be proficient in English. If you would feel better knowing how to rent a car in German (just in case), here are some words and phrases to use.

car	das Auto	dahs <u>ow</u>-toh
	der Wagen	day(r) <u>vah</u>-gen
rental car	der Mietwagen	day(r) <u>meet</u>-vah-gen
I would like to rent a car.	Ich möchte ein Auto mieten.	i^{ch} <u>mer^{ch}</u>-teh ine <u>ow</u>-toh <u>meet</u>-en
I have reserved a car.	Ich habe ein Auto reserviert.	i^{ch} <u>hah</u>-beh ine <u>ow</u>-toh Reh-zeh(r)-<u>vee(r)t</u>
from. . . until	von. . . bis	fon. . . bis
for __(2)__ people	für __(2)__ Personen	few(r) <u>(tsvy)</u> per-<u>zoh</u>-nen
insurance	die Versicherung	dee feh(r)-<u>zi^{ch}</u>-eR-ung
I also need insurance.	Ich brauche auch Versicherung.	i^{ch} <u>bRow</u>-$_{ch}$eh ow$_{ch}$ feh(r)-<u>zi^{ch}</u>-eR-ung
I have insurance.	Ich habe Versicherung.	i^{ch} <u>hah</u>-beh feh(r)-<u>zi^{ch}</u>-eR-ung

Driving a Car

gas station	die Tankstelle	dee <u>tahnk</u>-shtel-eh
self-service	Selbstbedienung (abbrev. SB)	zelbst-beh-<u>deen</u>-ung
Fill it up, please.	Volltanken, bitte.	<u>fol</u>-tahnk-en, <u>bit</u>-eh
__(20)__ Liters of gas	__(20)__ Liter Benzin	<u>(tvahn</u>-tsi^{ch}) <u>lee</u>-teh(r) ben-<u>tseen</u>
oil	das Öl	dahs erl
battery	die Batterie	dee bah-teh-<u>Ree</u>
tire	der Reifen	day(r) <u>Ry</u>-fen
broken	kaputt	kah-<u>put</u>
road entrance	die Einfahrt	dee <u>ine</u>-fah(r)t
road exit	die Ausfahrt	dee <u>ows</u>-fah(r)t
road toll	die Maut	dee mowt

Culture note—Car keys

Don't be alarmed if you have a switch-blade car key for your rental car. Push the button on the key fob and the key will pop out. The strange-looking engraved keys are supposed to be more secure than the traditional key-shaped ones.

Driving in Germany

Driving in Germany and Austria is not much different than driving in heavily populated areas of the U.S. There are some differences, however. Large stretches of German Autobahn have no speed limit (Austria does have an Autobahn speed limit of 130 kilometers per hour), and many German drivers live up to their aggressive driving reputation.

If you are driving in the passing lane and a car speeds up behind you and flashes its headlights, the driver wants you to pull back into the slow lane so he can pass. Traffic can be harrowing in and around cities, especially during rush hour. Regardless of where you are, the traffic flow can come to a sudden stop, leaving you caught in *Stau* (a traffic jam), possibly for hours on end. (You may notice the local drivers turning their cars off during long waits—at red lights, too. Part of the general emphasis on energy conservation.)

If you are used to driving in heavy urban traffic, you will likely adjust quickly to German driving, but to those of us from slower rural areas, the difference can be a shock. Not only is traffic usually dense and fast, but some basic rules of the road are different, and German drivers have no patience with uncertainty or ignorance on their highways and streets.

A cardinal rule in both countries is to *keep to the right!* Don't plan on cruising in the middle or far left lane unless you want to start an international incident. Bear in mind that it is actually illegal to pass on the right in Germany and Austria, and that drivers in the passing lane are required to let you in if you indicate that you want to pass (although they don't always try very hard to do so), and the insistence on keeping right becomes a little easier to understand. If people think you are driving too slowly in one of the left lanes, they might even emphatically point you over to the slow lane. Don't be offended if they do. Remember, this is their country, and they know the local practices better than we visitors do.

Off the Autobahn, state and local roads can be very narrow, often with no shoulder. Slower drivers often hug the right side of their lane, so faster drivers can pass down the middle of the road if they want to. This can happen even with an oncoming car, if that driver is also hugging the outside of the lane, resulting in a temporary three lanes of traffic on the two-lane road. If you are comfortable following a driver on a two-lane road but other drivers want to pass, you should leave a gap between your car and the one you are following, so faster drivers can leapfrog past you without having to pass at least two vehicles at the same time.

In town, some streets are so narrow that two cars can't pass each other—one must pull to the side and wait while the other one passes. With narrow streets and roads, hilly, twisting routes, and cars parked closely along the edge of streets, there is precious little room for driving error. Keep your wits about you, and try to avoid driving if you are not feeling alert.

Connect-the-dot navigation
In the United States, we are accustomed to following a particular highway in a particular direction until we reach our desired destination. This approach doesn't work in Germany and Austria. The roads and highways have numbers, but they don't include a general direction—north, south, east or west. Instead the emphasis is on towns and cities that lie in a particular direction on the road. Thus, if you are approaching the A3 Autobahn in Germany, your choice of direction may be Köln or Düsseldorf, not A3 South/A3 North. If you don't know where Köln and Düsseldorf are, it's pretty hard to know which direction to drive.

When driving in Germany and Austria, you need to think not about compass points, but about which cities are in the direction you want to travel. You may have no need to visit Düsseldorf, but if you want to go to Hamburg in the north, then you may need to follow the Düsseldorf sign. And then you may need to follow the sign to Münster after that. And then the sign to whatever comes next on the Autobahn. In Germany, don't think so much about driving from Point A to Point B as driving via half a dozen cities, checking each one off as you pass it, getting closer to your destination.

I can't help thinking of "connect the dot" games when I do this, and I call it connect-the-dot driving. When planning to drive, make sure you look at a map and see what other cities are in the direction you want to go, because that may be your only clue which on-ramp to take. Or, conversely, if you recognize a name on the sign (e.g., Frankfurt) and know that it is *not* the direction you want to drive, then you obviously choose the other direction.

Knowing how to "connect the dots" is especially important when you first arrive in the country and need to get your rental car out of the airport. The traffic will be heavy, the car will be unfamiliar, and you will be tired and disoriented from the long flight and unfamiliar surroundings. If you can identify a major city or two in the general direction you want to drive, you can at least get out of the airport mess while making progress toward your destination.

Don't get upset if you don't get the right road or right direction right away. That's awfully hard to do under those circumstances. It gets easier once you have had a little practice and a little sleep. Take your time, don't worry about a perfect route, and don't be afraid to ask for directions. Anything that gets you closer to your destination is good. It's all part of connecting the dots.

Culture note—Sidewalk parking

Most streets are narrow in German and Austrian towns. Don't be surprised if street parking is really "sidewalk" parking, with anywhere from one to all four wheels up on the sidewalk. If this is how others are parking, you may do it, also. Watch out for any signs limiting parking to certain hours, though. If in doubt about whether you may park as you have, ask at your hotel.

Culture note—Navi-System

It seems that almost all Germans and Austrians drive with a GPS system these days. Known as *Navigation* or a *Navi-System*, these gadgets are beloved driving aids. After you drive around in circles in a city sometime, trying to locate your hotel, you may decide that it's worth the extra expense to rent one with your car. Otherwise, you can certainly get by with maps and good driving instructions from an Internet site, such as *www.viamichelin.com*. It helps immensely if you have a partner to assist with navigation. If you are driving alone and covering unfamiliar territory (I've been there, and it wasn't fun), you might seriously consider renting a *Navi-System*, or even buying one in Europe, if your stay will be long.

Driving requirements

All occupants in a car are legally required to use their seat belts. In Austria, drivers must have their headlights on at all times. If you drive on the Autobahn in Austria, you need to buy a toll sticker (*eine Vignette*), available at gas stations. And if you have a child along, you may need to have a booster seat, even though your child is no longer required to use one in your home state. Children younger than 12 must sit in the back seat.

Speed limits and photographs

For all their fabled fondness of rules, German drivers don't respect speed limits. Violate them at your own risk, though. Many areas are now overseen with radar, and speeders may face a sudden flash of light as their picture is automatically taken for a speeding ticket. (They are *geblitzt*, in German, literally "flashed," and everyone knows what it means. A fine for speeding.) Construction zones are particularly likely to have radar control.

In all fairness, though, it can be hard to figure out what the speed limit is in any particular place. If you catch a speed limit sign (black number posted on a round white sign within a red circle), it's not so hard, but the limit could soon change, and if you miss the sign, you're out of luck. (A white circular sign with a set of diagonal lines indicates when you pass the end of the speed zone.)

Regular, posted speed limits are overridden by temporary postings on the Autobahn indicating lower limits because of heavy traffic. And construction areas will also have lower limits posted. This is all mixed up with stretches of the Autobahn that don't have *any* speed limit. Even Germans sometimes don't know what the speed limit is supposed to be if they are driving on unfamiliar roads. I admit, I'm a cautious person, but I prefer not to risk the possibility of a ticket (the police can track you through your rental agency), and I stay within striking distance of the posted limit. There's no shame in being passed by faster drivers, and there's much to be said in favor of a more relaxed approach to driving.

Exit and destination signs

Autobahn exit signs are indicated by the word *Ausfahrt* or the symbol of a side arrow splitting off from the main arrow. Exit numbers in Germany are indicated just as a number within a white circle on the large blue Autobahn signs. Exit numbers in Germany do not correspond with the kilometer marking (e.g., exit 17 could be 40 kilometers from exit 16).

Destination signs on highways in Germany and Austria are oriented differently than in the United States. Rather than the closest city being listed highest on the sign, with increasing distance to cities listed lower on the sign, German signs do the reverse. You need to read the sign from bottom to top if you want to get the listings in order of nearest town to farthest one. Try to imagine that the sign is lying on the ground in front of you, in which case the nearest city listing indicates the nearest city. The same orientation holds true for exit signs—if more than one exit is listed on the sign, the bottom listing is the one you will come to first.

Culture note—Zipper merge

If you are required to merge in traffic, the usual practice is to form a "zipper" (*Reißverschluss*). You are usually not supposed to merge until actually at the merging point, when cars from each lane are expected to alternate, like the teeth on a closing zipper.

Culture note—Keep right! Or not. . .

Germans and Austrians are adamant about keeping to the right lane as much as possible when you drive. (Not them, mind you, but *you*.) While you should usually *not* cruise in a left lane, if you are on a multi-lane section of Autobahn and the right lane is clogged with big trucks and campers, you can get away with it, as long as you keep up with the speed of traffic in that lane. If you aren't comfortable driving as fast as others, you should stick with the slow lane.

Rest stops
Rest stops are fairly frequent along the Autobahn. They may be labeled *Raststation* or *Rasthof* or *Autohof*. A road sign marked with a large P indicates that parking is available (if you need to stretch your legs or check your map), and WC ("water closet") indicates that toilets are available. Don't expect a lot at the simple roadside stops. The bathroom may be smelly, with no seat, no soap, and possibly no toilet paper. If you need to go, though, you need to go. Larger rest stops will have gas stations, restaurants, even hotels. Signs on the Autobahn should indicate what services the upcoming stop has. The sign might also indicate how many kilometers until the next rest stop with a gas station, if you are concerned about timing your refueling stops.

City center signs
If you are ready to leave the Autobahn or highway and want to get to the city center, the route will be marked by the words *Zentrum* (center) or *Stadtmitte* (city center) or by a bull's-eye or large dot. The *Altstadt* indicates the "old city."

Roundabouts
Many traditional road intersections have been replaced with roundabouts (*Kreisverkehr*). Make sure you yield upon entering one, then you may drive around as many times as you need to. I quite like the roundabout approach. If I want to double check the signs to get the right exit, I can do so without holding up the other drivers. Just go around again.

Right-of-way

At intersections on a highway—this happens a lot when the road runs though a town or city—you can determine you have the right-of-way if the road you are on has a sign that shows a square yellow diamond on a white background. If you need to yield, a white sign will show the main road curving in front of your road.

Traffic signals

Traffic signals in Germany and Austria warn you when they are about to change from green to yellow or from red to green. In Germany, if you see a green light and suddenly the yellow one joins it, that means the light will soon turn to yellow. In Austria, the green light blinks four times as a warning before it turns to yellow. If the light is yellow, you should not enter the intersection. When the red light is nearing the end of its cycle, the yellow light turns on, too, indicating that drivers can prepare to take off—and they do, as soon as the light turns green, so don't dawdle or you'll get honked at.

Right turns are generally not allowed on a red light, unless there is an extra green arrow posted right next to the light, pointing to the right.

At the Train Station/On the Train

Train schedules

At the train station, you will find posters that list train arrivals and departures. Arrivals are listed under *Ankunft* and departures and destinations are under *Abfahrt*. If you are meeting someone who is getting off a train, you want to look at the *Ankunft* listings. More likely, though, you will be concerned only with departures, that is, *Abfahrt*.

The *Abfahrt* board has several columns across it. This is how you read the information. *Zeit* means *time* and indicates the time of departure. (Note that these listings will use the 24-hour clock.) *Zug* indicates the number of the train you want to take. *Richtung* means "direction" (or it could say *nach*, which means *to*) and indicates destinations for a particular train. This is probably the first column you will want to look at, to find out which trains go where you want to. The arrival time for each destination is included after the city name. The next column is *Gleis* or *Bahnsteig* and tells you which track or platform to go to in order to board your train.

Pay attention to how long it takes to get to your destination— some trains are much faster than others. It's quite possible that a later-leaving train will arrive at your destination sooner, if it's a faster train.

A couple types of regional trains are identified as RE (*Regionalexpress*) and RB (*Regionalbahn*). The RE train is faster and will typically list all its stops on the *Abfahrt* board. The RB train is slower and will often list just its final stop, to indicate direction, but will then stop at all the little stations along the route. Not all smaller trains run on the weekends. Check at the counter or the information desk, if you are uncertain about one you want to take.

Buying train tickets

Buy your train ticket and make any reservations you want at a window bearing a *Fahrkarten* sign. If you will be traveling within the country, you will want the *Inland* window, if there is one. For travel out of the country, you will want *Ausland*, if such a window is available. (*Land* means *country*.) Ask for "eine Fahrkarte nach _____." A one-way ticket is *einfach*. Roundtrip is *hin und zurück*.

Travel tip: You can investigate train schedules and ticket prices from the comfort of your home computer. Information on German rail service (the *Deutsche Bahn*) can be found at *www.bahn. de*. If you click the link for "International Guests," you will find information in English. Austrian rail service (ÖBB) information is at *www.oebb.at*, and Swiss railway information is available at *www. sbb.ch*. Both the Austrian and the Swiss sites let you choose English at the top of the page. These sites can provide you with information about trains in other countries, too.

Train schedule vocabulary

The following table is useful if you need to investigate train schedules in German.

Fahrplan	schedule	anderes	other
von	from	Dauer	duration
nach	to	umsteigen	change trains
über	via	Rückfahrt	return trip
Uhrzeit	time	suchen	search
Datum	date	Preis	price
morgen	tomorrow	neue Anfrage	new search

Luggage lockers

Luggage lockers (*Schließfächer*) or luggage storage (*Gepäckaufbewahrung*) might be available at the train station, if you don't want to haul your baggage around with you. Fees are very reasonable.

Delays

While trains are quite punctual, delays are not uncommon. If you see or hear the word *Verspätung* in connection with your train, that means it is delayed. If an announcement comes over the loudspeaker while you are standing on the platform waiting for your train to arrive, and everyone around you groans, you can count on it that a delay has just been announced.

First or second class

Your train ticket is for either a first- or second-class coach. Make sure you sit in the right kind of car. Classes are marked on the outside of the trains, next to the doors, as well as inside the train. There will usually be a display case out on the platform with diagrams of major trains, listing what kinds of cars will be where when the train pulls in. If your train is listed, find the type of car you want and then stand in the area where that car is supposed to stop. Use the letters hanging from the roof above you as guides. Those letters correspond to the letters displayed on the diagram.

Toiletten

Each train car has bathrooms near the main doors, marked *Toilette*. A small sign next to the handle will show whether the room is *besetzt* (occupied) or *frei* (vacant). The sign will display a red or green color block to indicate availability.

Because of the way some train toilets flush (onto the track), you should not use the bathroom when the train is at a station.

6   Emergencies and Additional Vocabulary

Numbers (100-1000, by 100)

Let's take on the last of German numbers—hundreds and thousands. Again, review the previous number sections to store them a little more deeply in your memory before starting this new section.

100	(ein)-hundert	*(ine)-hoon-deh(r)t*
200	zwei-hundert	*tsvy-hoon-deh(r)t*
300	drei-hundert	*dRy-hoon-deh(r)t*
400	vier-hundert	*fee(r)-hoon-deh(r)t*
500	fünf-hundert	*fewnf-hoon-deh(r)t*
600	sechs-hundert	*ze*^{*ch*}*s-hoon-deh(r)t*
700	sieben-hundert	*zee-ben-hoon-deh(r)t*
800	acht-hundert	*ah*_{*cht*}*-hoon-deh(r)t*
900	neun-hundert	*noyn-hoon-deh(r)t*
1 000	(ein)-tausend	*(ine)-tow-zent*

You now have the building blocks to build numbers up to (and past) one thousand. See how large numbers are put together. Again, these examples have hyphens between different parts of the words to make them easier to read. Correctly written, each German number is one long word without breaks.

264	zwei-hundert-vier-und-sechzig
437	vier-hundert-sieben-und-dreißig
859	acht-hundert-neun-und-fünfzig
705	sieben-hundert-fünf
4 173	vier-tausend-ein-hundert-drei-und-siebzig

Reality check: If you really hate learning numbers, you can probably get by just fine without the high numbers. Concentrate on being able to count comfortably from one to twenty (or, better, from one to one hundred) and then make do if you need to communicate larger numbers.

Culture note—Commas and decimal points

In German numbers, commas and periods are used differently than in the American system. A comma is used to indicate decimals (where we would use a period), and a period is used to indicate thousands (where we would use a comma).

American	3,576.90
German	3.576,90

You will see the comma most frequently in prices. For example, *7,40 Euro* means seven euros and 40 cents.

Exercise 6.1
Can you write out these numbers in German without looking at the list above?

1.	165	7.	328
2.	647	8.	783
3.	812	9.	479
4.	231	10.	1 014
5.	597	11.	3 285
6.	956		

Answers: 1) (ein)hundert-fünf-und-sechzig, 2) sechs-hundert-sieben-und-vierzig, 3) acht-hundert-zwölf, 4) zwei-hundert-ein-und-dreißig, 5) fünf-hundert-sieben-und-neunzig, 6) neun-hundert-sechs-und-fünfzig, 7) drei-hundert-acht-und-zwanzig, 8) sieben-hundert-drei-und-achtzig, 9) vier-hundert-neun-und-siebzig, 10) (ein)tausend-vierzehn, 11) drei-tausend-zwei-hundert-fünf-und-achtzig

---

Culture note—Germs and hygiene

Many Germans and Austrians think Americans are obsessed with germs and personal hygiene. Don't expect to find hand sanitizers available, or even consistently stocked soap dispensers. If things like hand sanitizer or wet wipes are important to you, you should take your own supplies along. The Germans and Austrians I know generally follow the philosophy that exposure to everyday germs helps strengthen the immune system.

Grammar—Commands and questions

Here's another grammar "freebie." You can get by without it, but it costs almost no effort to learn and might help you understand better what people say to you: The formal command form and question form are the same.

> Nehmen Sie Reiseschecks? (Do you take traveler's checks?)
> Nehmen Sie ein Stück Torte! (Take a piece of cake!)
> Gehen Sie ins Theater? (Are you going to the theater?)
> Gehen Sie nach rechts und dann geradeaus!
>   (Go to the right and then straight ahead!)

Exercise 6.2

Match the question or command in column A with the correct response in column B.

A	B
1. Haben Sie Zimmer frei?	A. Nein, ich trinke lieber (rather) Saft.
2. Wo ist der Hauptbahnhof?	B. Nein, sie (it) ist zu teuer!
3. Trinken Sie gern Wein?	C. Gehen Sie nach rechts bis zum Park und dann nach links.
4. Nehmen Sie ein Stück (piece) Torte!	D. Nein, wir sind leider (unfortunately) voll.
5. Kaufen Sie die Kuckucksuhr!	E. Danke schön. Ich esse gern Schokolade.

Answers: 1) D, 2) C, 3) A, 4) E, 5) B

Emergencies

Odds are that you won't encounter any emergencies abroad, but if you do, you might not have time to look up how to say something. Learning some basic emergency vocabulary can be a life-saving investment. If nothing else, at least learn how to say "Help!"

Help!	Hilfe!	_hil_-feh!
Pay attention! Watch out!	Paß auf!/Passen Sie auf!	pahs owf! _pah_-sen zee owf!
Be careful! Watch out!	Vorsicht!	_foh(r)_-zi ^{ch}t!
Go away!	Geh weg!/Gehen Sie weg!	gay vek! _gay_-en zee vek!
danger to life	Lebensgefahr!	_lay_-bens-geh-fah(r)
Fire!	Feuer!	_foy_-eh(r)
hospital	das Krankenhaus	dahs _kRahnk_-en-hows
telephone	das Telefon	dahs _teh_-leh-fohn
cell phone	das Handy	dahs _hen_-dee
Call ___!	Rufen Sie ___!	_Roo_-fen zee ___
an ambulance	einen Krankenwagen	_ine_-en _kRahnk_-en-vah-gen
a doctor	einen Arzt	_ine_-en ah(r)ts
the police	die Polizei	dee poh-li-_tsy_
the fire department	die Feuerwehr	dee _foy_-eh(r)-vay(r)

Culture note—Crime and drunkenness

Tourists are not in great danger of being victims of crime, other than possible (but unlikely) petty theft in some urban areas. Watch out for pickpockets. As in any other country, do whatever you can to keep your valuables safe and hard to reach.

Unfortunately, running across public drunkenness is not out of the question, especially in areas with high unemployment. Drug use is also not uncommon in some places. If you feel at all uneasy about any individuals or groups you encounter, follow your instincts and play it safe. Even though nothing untoward is likely to happen, you may avoid an unpleasant confrontation.

Exercise 6.3

How would you say the following in German? Remember, if masculine nouns are in the accusative case (see pp. 98 for a review), then der/ein changes to den/einen.

1. Call the police!

2. Help!

3. Call an ambulance!

4. Call a doctor!

5. Where is a telephone?

6. Watch out!

7. Fire!

Answers: 1) Rufen Sie die Polizei! 2) Hilfe! 3) Rufen Sie einen Krankenwagen! 4) Rufen Sie einen Arzt! 5) Wo ist ein Telefon? 6) Vorsicht!/Paß auf!/Passen Sie auf! 7) Feuer!

Culture note—Prostitution

Prostitution is legal in many places in Germany and Austria. Legal prostitutes are registered, taxed and closely monitored by health officials. They often work in brothels or *Stundenhotels* ("hourly hotels"). Streetwalkers are less likely to be legal and monitored.

If you choose a perfectly nice, well-priced hotel in a less-than-desirable area of town (often indicated by the presence of sex shops or pornographic bookstores or movie theaters), you may not want to wander around the neighborhood after dark. During the day is not likely to be any problem, though.

Public telephones and calling home

It seems that everyone in Germany and Austria now has a cell phone, called a *Handy* in German. While very convenient for the locals, this prevalence of cell phones spells trouble for the tourist who wants to use a public phone. With such a low demand for public telephones, few of them are available anymore. And many phone booths that are still around are strictly for emergency calls and can't even be used for standard phone calls. If you find a booth that allows regular phone calls, you will probably need a German or Austrian phone card to operate it, and the only reliable place you can buy those now is at the post office. You can also place international calls from a booth in the post office, but you need to work around the post office's business hours, then.

If you have a phone in your hotel room, you can probably either call directly to the United States or even use a U.S.-based phone card. Be aware, however, that international calling rates can be very expensive—especially from hotels—and not all hotel phones will let you dial the toll-free number necessary to access your U.S.-based phone service. (Phone companies such as AT&T have a different toll-free number in each country, so check with your service to get the correct number before you leave.)

During an exceptionally weak exchange rate, I once faced a hotel phone bill of over $110 for a couple of long conversations, not realizing that the rate in Austria was substantially higher than what I had recently paid in Germany. And this was *after* checking at the desk before calling and being assured that the calling rates at the hotel were good (*günstig*). I should have checked more thoroughly—placed a short call and then checked on the charge, for example—but it was late, I was exhausted from a long day's drive, I had a child along, and I had been out of communication for the better part of a week. Learn from my expensive mistake! I should have had my husband *call us back* in our hotel room.

So what's the best way to contact home from Germany or Austria? You can ask your hotel reception for advice on phoning, but they might not be familiar with the best options for calling the United States. You can take your chances with direct dialing, but keep conversations short. You can look into buying a German or Austrian international phone card, if you've had luck spotting public telephone booths. You could buy a European cell phone and the minutes to use it. Who knows what's best?? Telecommunications change so rapidly that what I have written here could be out of date by the time you intend to travel. A good way to get current information is to check a travel guide book that updates its information annually. I know that the Rick Steves' guides to Germany and Austria, for example, include good overviews of current phone options and costs.

Culture note—The telephone ring

Phones ring differently in Germany than in America. If you place a call to Germany or Austria, how do you know it has gone through? A long "doo" sound that slowly repeats means that the phone is ringing on the other end. A series of short, fast doo-doo-doos indicates that the line is busy. A musically rising, repeated doo-doo-doo means something was wrong with the number you dialed and the phone you are on can't complete the call.

When someone answers a private phone in Germany or Austria, they usually either say their last name, or sometimes they rattle off their phone number in greeting. Be prepared for either one.

Culture note—Fitness

People have asked me how Germans and Austrians generally stay so slim and fit, compared to the average American, even when they have "all those sausages, potatoes and beer." I think it boils down to the obvious reasons—more activity and fewer calories.

First, walking is still part of the typical European's life—walking to public transportation, walking to shops, walking up stairs because there are fewer elevators and escalators. Bicycling is also a popular form of transportation, and bike paths and lanes abound.

Second, Germans and Austrians usually have two modest meals a day, with only one larger "hot" meal. The two modest meals are both sandwich-based. It's not unusual to see almost the same bread, meat, cheese, fruits and vegetables on the table at breakfast and at supper.

The food is fresh, tasty, healthy and filling, but I suspect people eat less of it because there's less variety from meal to meal. I have the impression that Germans and Austrians feed their hunger more than their palate. They don't overdo things. And, certainly, not eating dessert with meals helps keep the calorie count down, too.

At the doctor / At the pharmacy

No one wants to get sick or hurt while away from home (and if you do, your healthcare worker will probably know English), but there's peace of mind in knowing some rudimentary health vocabulary.

It hurts here.	Es tut hier weh.	*es toot hee(r) vay*
I'm sick.	Ich bin krank.	*i^{ch} bin kRahnk*
I've vomited.	Ich habe mich übergeben.	*i^{ch} hah-beh mi^{ch} ew-beh(r)-gay-ben*
I'm bleeding.	Ich blute.	*i^{ch} bloo-teh*
I have ___.	Ich habe ___.	*i^{ch} hah-beh ___*
a fever	Fieber	*fee-beh(r)*
constipation	Verstopfung	*feh(r)-shtop-fung*
diarrhea	Durchfall	*du(r)^{ch}-fahl*
a headache	Kopfschmerzen	*kopf-shmeh(r)t-sen*
a stomach ache	Magenschmerzen	*mah-gen-shmeh(r)t-sen*
a cold	eine Erkältung	*ine-eh eh(r)-kel-tung*

Note: If you have a health condition, know how to say it in German, just as a precaution.

I'm a diabetic.	Ich bin Diabetiker/-in.	*i^{ch} bin dee-ah-beh-tee-keh(r) (male) /-kehR-in (female)*
My blood pressure is too high.	Mein Blutdruck ist zu hoch.	*mine bloot-dRuk ist tsoo hoh$_{ch}$*
I have a weak heart.	Ich habe ein schwaches Herz.	*i^{ch} hah-beh ine shvah-$_{ch}$es heh(r)ts*
I have asthma.	Ich habe Asthma.	*i^{ch} hah-beh ahst-mah*
I'm allergic to ___.	Ich bin allergisch gegen ___.	*i^{ch} bin ah-leh(r)-gish gay-gen ___*
nuts	Nüsse	*new-seh*
penicillin	Penizillin	*pen-ee-tsi-leen*
strawberries	Erdbeeren	*eh(r)t-bay-Ren*
feathers	Federn	*fay-deh(r)n*

Culture note—Drugstores and pharmacies

Drugstores and pharmacies are separate stores in Germany and Austria. A drugstore (*eine Drogerie*) carries toiletries and other non-drug "drugstore" items. If you want any drugs, including over-the-counter ones, you need to visit a pharmacy (*eine Apotheke*). It's possible to get herbal remedies in a *Drogerie*, but if you are not feeling well, you are better off visiting an *Apotheke*, where drugs are regulated and trained personnel can recommend treatment.

Body Parts

My ___ hurts.	Mein ___ tut weh.	*mine ___ toot vay*
arm	Arm	*ah(r)m*
back	Rücken	*Rew-ken*
bone	Knochen	*kno_{ch}-en*
chest	meine Brust	*mine-eh bRust*
ear	Ohr	*oh(r)*
eye	Auge	*ow-geh*
finger	Finger	*fing-eh(r)*
foot	Fuß	*foos*
hand	meine Hand	*mine-eh hahnt*
head	Kopf	*kopf*
stomach	Magen	*mah-gen*
heart	Herz	*heh(r)ts*
jaw	Kiefer	*kee-feh(r)*
knee	Knie	*k-nee*
leg	Bein	*bine*
lung	meine Lunge	*mine-eh lung-eh*
mouth	Mund	*munt*
muscle	Muskel	*mus-kel*
neck, throat	Hals	*hahls*
nose	meine Nase	*mine-eh nah-zeh*
shoulder	meine Schulter	*mine-eh shool-teh(r)*
skin	meine Haut	*mine-eh howt*
tonsils	Meine Mandeln tun weh.	*mine-eh mahn-deln toon vay*

Culture note—Cleanliness

One of the pleasures of traveling in Germany and Austria is marveling at how clean and orderly those lands generally are. Windows sparkle. Sidewalks are swept and front stoops regularly scrubbed. Gardens and hedges are neat and tidy. Most homes, hotels, and restaurants are immaculate. Standards may be relaxing a bit with the younger generation, but in general, there's a great appreciation of cleanliness and order.

Medication

medication	das Medikament	dahs meh-dee-kah-_ment_
prescription	das Rezept	dahs Ray-_tsept_
aspirin	das Aspirin	dahs _ahs_-pee-Reen
decongestant spray	das Nasenspray	dahs _nah_-zen-shpRay
eye drops	die Augentropfen	dee _ow_-gen-tRop-fen
antihistamine	das Antihistamin	dahs ahn-tee-hist-ah-_meen_
cough medicine	das Hustenmittel	dahs _hoos_-ten-mit-el
antacid	das Antazidum	dahs ahn-tah-_tsee_-dum

Additional Vocabulary

Travelers frequently want to know how to say things beyond the bare necessities. This section includes three very common topics: family, occupations and the weather.

Family

family	die Familie	dee fah-_meel_-yah
parents	die Eltern	dee _el_-teh(r)n
father	der Vater	day(r) _fah_-teh(r)
mother	die Mutter	dee _mut_-eh(r)
child	das Kind	dahs kint
children	die Kinder	dee _kin_-deh(r)
son	der Sohn	day(r) zohn

daughter	die Tochter	dee <u>to</u>_{ch}-teh(r)
siblings	die Geschwister	dee geh-<u>shvis</u>-teh(r)
brother	der Bruder	day(r) <u>bRoo</u>-deh(r)
sister	die Schwester	dee <u>shves</u>-teh(r)
grandparents	die Großeltern	dee <u>gRohs</u>-el-teh(r)n
grandfather	der Großvater	day(r) <u>gRohs</u>-fah-teh(r)
grandmother	die Großmutter	dee <u>gRohs</u>-mut-eh(r)
grandchildren	die Enkel	dee <u>enk</u>-el
grandson	der Enkel	day(r) <u>enk</u>-el
granddaughter	die Enkelin	dee <u>enk</u>-el-in
uncle	der Onkel	day(r) <u>onk</u>-el
aunt	die Tante	dee <u>tahn</u>-teh
nephew	der Neffe	day(r) <u>nef</u>-eh
niece	die Nichte	dee <u>ni</u>^{ch}-teh
male cousin	der Cousin	day(r) ku-<u>zeng</u>
female cousin	die Cousine	dee ku-<u>zee</u>-neh

Culture note—Multi-generational living

It's not unusual to find two or three generations of a family sharing a house. Property is very expensive in Germany and Austria, and it often makes good financial sense for families to share the burden. There are other advantages to this relationship, as well, as the different generations can help each other with child care, cooking, housework or yardwork, for example. Some people with large houses choose to rent part of them out, either as apartments or as *Ferienwohnungen,* "vacation apartments." All of these choices make sense for the people who make them—they are *günstige* arrangements.

---

man or husband	der Mann	day(r) mahn
woman or wife	die Frau	dee fRow
girl	das Mädchen	dahs <u>mayd</u>-^{ch}en
boy	der Junge	day(r) <u>yung</u>-eh
baby	das Baby	dahs <u>bay</u>-bee
I'm ___.	Ich bin ___.	i^{ch} bin ___

married	verheiratet	*feh(r)-hy-Rah-tet*
single	ledig	*lay-di ch*
separated	getrennt	*geh-tRent*
divorced	geschieden	*geh-shee-den*
widowed	verwitwet	*feh(r)-vit-vet*
____ is deceased.	____ ist gestorben.	____ *ist geh-shto(r)-ben*
My husband	Mein Mann	*mine mahn*
My wife	Meine Frau	*mine-eh fRow*
My grandfather	Mein Großvater	*mine gRohs-vah-teh(r)*
pet	das Haustier	*dahs hows-tee(r)*
cat	die Katze	*dee kaht-seh*
dog	der Hund	*day(r) hoont*
fish	der Fisch	*day(r) fish*
bird	der Vogel	*day(r) foh-gehl*

Exercise 6.4

How would you answer these questions in German?

1. Sind Sie verheiratet?

2. Wie heißt Ihr (your) Mann/Ihre Frau?

3. Haben Sie Kinder?

4. Haben Sie Enkel? Wie viele?

5. Haben Sie ein Haustier?

Answers: 1) Ja, ich bin verheiratet./Nein, ich bin nicht verheiratet./Nein, ich bin ledig. 2) Er/Sie heißt _____. 3) Ja, ich habe Kinder./Ja, ich habe _____ Kinder. /Ja, ich habe eine Tochter/einen Sohn./Nein, ich habe keine Kinder. 4) Ja, ich habe Enkel. Drei./Ja, ich habe drei Enkel./Nein, ich habe keine Enkel. 5) Ja, ich habe ein/eine/einen _____./Nein, ich habe kein Haustier.

Reality check: So far in this book, we have focused on using "I" and "you," with a little bit of "we" thrown in. The next couple of grammar sections introduce ways to talk about *other* people— he/she/it (called third-person singular) and *du*, the informal "you" (called second-person informal singular). These brief sections are included so you have the basics about these forms, in case you want to talk about your friends or relatives, for example, or you want to address young people or relatives with the more-appropriate informal. If you "don't have time to mess with this stuff," then don't. Just stick with "you" and "I" and skip ahead to Occupations or Weather.

Grammar—Third-person singular (he/she/it)

If you want to talk about other people—your husband, your grandmother, your child—then you need to know the third-person singular verb form, that is, the form of the verb that goes with *he*, *she* or *it*.

Some common verbs

	gehen	sagen	arbeiten
ich	geh-e	sag-e	arbeit-e
Sie	geh-en	sag-en	arbeit-en
er/sie/es	geh-t	sag-t	arbeit-et

First, let's learn the pronouns. *He* is *er* (pronounced like "air" in English, but backing off the "r" sound), *she* is *sie* ("zee"), and *it* is *es* ("ess").

For many verbs, you form the he/she/it form by taking the stem of the verb and adding a *-t* or sometimes an *-et* ending. For example, the verb *gehen* (to go) has the stem *geh-*. Add a *-t* ending, and you get the form *geht*, as in *er geht* (he goes). Or take the verb *sagen* (to say), remove the *-en* ending and add a *-t* to the stem and you get *sagt*, as in *sie sagt* (she says).

When the verb stem ends in a *-t* or *-d*, then you need to add an *-et* to the verb stem, simply to make it easier to say: *er arbeitet* (he works), for example. Many German verbs follow this straightforward pattern. You may recognize the following: *gehen* (to go), *sagen* (to say), *machen* (to make or to do), *kommen* (to come), *reisen* (to travel), *heißen* (to be called), *schreiben* (to write), *wohnen* (to live).

Common verbs that require a stem change

	sprechen	schlafen	laufen
ich	sprech-e	schlaf-e	lauf-e
Sie	sprech-en	schlaf-en	lauf-en
er/sie/es	sprich-t	schläf-t	läuf-t

There are many other common verbs that behave just fine in the *ich* and *Sie* forms, but surprise us in the *er/sie/es* form by requiring a stem change. That means that when you use the German verb to go with he, she or it, the vowel in the stem changes along with the end of the verb. For example, you would like to say that your daughter speaks German very well. The female pronoun is *sie*. Check. The verb is *sprechen*. Check. But what comes next? We know to replace the *-en* ending with a *-t*, and that gets us to "sprecht," but it's not enough. We also need to change the *e* in "sprech" to an *i*, giving us the correct form of *spricht: Sie spricht gut Deutsch*. Other common changes in third-person singular include going from an *e* to an *ie* (*empfehlen* to *er empfiehlt*), *a* changing to *ä* (*schlafen* to *es schläft*) or *au* changing to *äu* (*laufen* to *sie läuft*), but there are many others, too.

Grammar—Second-person informal, singular (du)

	gehen	sagen	arbeiten
er/sie/es	geh-t	sag-t	arbeit-et
du	geh-st	sag-st	arbeit-est

	sprechen	schlafen	laufen
er/sie/es	sprich-t	schläf-t	läuf-t
du	sprich-st	schläf-st	läuf-st

If you are going to learn he/she/it forms, you might as well learn the informal "you" form (*du*), because they are very similar. With many regular verbs, such as *gehen* and *sagen*, you take the stem of the verb, such as *geh-* and add an *-st* ending to get the *du* form: *du* *gehst*. With *sagen*, you would get *du sagst*. So, to ask "Where do you come from?" you would end up with *Woher kommst du?*

As discussed above, though, many verbs change their stem vowels when in the *er/sie/es* form. The same change is evident in the *du* form; you just add the ending -*st*. So while "he speaks" is *er spricht*, "you speak" (informal) is *du sprichst*. Or we could make a question from it: *Sprichst du Englisch?* Easy enough. But how do you know whether a verb changes its stem in these forms? Any dictionary will list irregular German verb forms. I include irregular forms in the dictionary entries at the back of this book.

Some irregular verbs

	haben	sein
ich	habe	bin
Sie	haben	sind
er/sie/es	hat	ist
du	hast	bist

A couple of the most common verbs behave in "irregular" ways and don't act the way we expect them to. The verbs *haben* (to have) and *sein* (to be) don't follow the rules for third-person singular or the informal *du*. To say he/she/it *has* something, use the form *hat*—*er hat, sie hat, es hat*. (Pronounced like "hot," not "hat.") To say he/she/it *is*, the German form is *ist*—*er ist, sie ist, es ist*. The informal "you are" is *du bist*, and the informal "you have" is *du hast*. These forms are so common that you quickly get comfortable with them, even though they are irregular.

Reality check: People will probably be able to figure out what you are saying even if you don't make these he/she/it stem changes. "Sie sprecht gut Deutsch" will get the message across just fine. When you are aiming at communication and don't have much time to study, you can overlook these finer points. *Do*, however, make sure you learn the correct forms for "he/she has" and "he/she is." Those can be quite useful.

Culture note—Traveling with children

I have had wonderful experiences traveling in Germany and Austria with children. Locals have generally reacted very warmly. Hotels and restaurants are well prepared to serve children, and there are often price reductions for children in hotels and on public transportation. Children (and older students with picture IDs) usually receive free or reduced admission at museums, tourist attractions and performances. It is greatly appreciated, of course, when children are well-mannered and relatively quiet. If you rent a car, make sure you get the necessary car seats or boosters from your rental agency.

When visiting Germans and Austrians, don't be surprised if they have small gifts for your children. It's also common practice to *bring* a small gift or two for any children whose families *you* visit. Popular gifts include books and small toys, with modest jewelry and stationery supplies also appropriate.

Occupations

What do you do (for a job)?	Was machen Sie (beruflich)?	vahs *mah*-ch*en zee (beh-*Roof*-li ch)?
I'm [a(n)] ___.	Ich bin ___.	i ch bin ___
My wife is [a(n)] ___.	Meine Frau ist ___.	*mine*-eh fRow ist ___
My husband is [a(n)] ___.	Mein Mann ist ___.	mine mahn ist ___
accountant	Buchhalter/-in	*boo*ch-hahl-teh(r)/-in
architect	Architekt/-in	ah(r)-ch ee-*tekt*/-in
artist	Künstler/-in	*kewnst*-leh(r)/-in
businessman	Geschäftsmann	geh-*shefts*-mahn
businesswoman	Geschäftsfrau	geh-*shefts*-fRow
carpenter	Zimmermann	*tsim*-eh(r)-mahn
computer scientist	Informatiker/-in	in-fo(r)-*mah*-tee-keh(r)/-in
doctor	Arzt/Ärztin	ahrtst/*eh(r)t*-stin
engineer	Ingenieur/-in	in-zheh-*new(r)*/-in

farmer	Bauer/Bäuerin	_bow_-eh(r)/_boy_-eh(r)-in
housewife	Hausfrau	_hows_-fRow
laborer	Arbeiter/-in	_ah(r)_-bite-eh(r)/-in
lawyer	Rechtsanwalt/-anwältin	_Rechts_-ahn-valt/-ahn-velt-in
manager	Leiter/-in	_ly_-teh(r)/-in
mechanic	Mechaniker/-in	meh-_ch__ah_-nee-keh(r)/-in
minister	Pfarrer/-in	_pfah_-Reh(r)/-in
musician	Musiker/-in	_moo_-zee-keh(r)/-in
nun	Nonne	_non_-eh
nurse (female)	Krankenschwester	_kRahnk_-en-shves-teh(r)
nurse (male)	Krankenpfleger	_kRahnk_-en-pflay-geh(r)
pilot	Pilot/-in	pee-_loht_/-tin
plumber	Klempner/-in	_klemp_-neh(r)/-in
priest	Priester	_pRee_-steh(r)
professor	Professor/-in	proh-_fes_-o(r)/proh-fes-_oh_-Rin
retired	Rentner/-in	_Rent_-neh(r)/-in
salesperson	Verkäufer/-in	feh(r)-_koy_-feh(r)/-in
sales representative	Vertreter/-in	feh(r)-_tRay_-teh(r)/-in
scientist	Wissenschaftler/-in	_vis_-en-shahft-leh(r)/-in
secretary	Sekretär/-in	zek-Reh-_tay(r)_/-in
stay-home dad	Hausmann	_hows_-mahn
student (K-12)	Schüler/-in	_shew_-leh(r)/-in
student (university)	Student/-in	shtoo-_dent_/-in
teacher	Lehrer/-in	_lay(r)_-eR/-in
writer	Schriftsteller/-in	_shRift_-shtel-eh(r)/-in
unemployed	arbeitslos	_ah(r)_-bites-lohs
self-employed	Selbständiger/Selbständige	_zelp_-shten-dig-eh(r) / _zelp_-shten-dig-eh

Note: You don't use _a_ or _an_ when naming your occupation in German. _Ich bin Lehrerin_ is literally, "I am teacher," but sounds as natural and correct in German as "I am a teacher" does to

Americans. *Ich bin Klempner. Er ist Priester. Sie ist Künstlerin.* All are correct German. Try to resist the urge to insert an *ein* or *eine.*

If, for some reason, you wanted to talk about *the* waitress or worker or whatever, simply add *der* (or *den*, if it's in the accusative case) before a masculine job word or *die* before a feminine one. Most occupations have an ending to indicate whether the position is held by a man or a women. The feminine ending of *-in* is frequently added to the "base" form, which usually indicates a man. For example, a male accountant is a *Buchhalter*, but a female accountant is a *Buchhalterin*. The added ending for feminine form is indicated by a /*-in* after the base form of the word.

Grammar—Possessive adjectives

When talking about your family, you often want to use a possessive, usually *my* or *our*, to identify your relatives. (My cousin lives in Berlin. Our daughter is a student.) Or you may hear others talking about possession and will want to understand what they are saying. (May I have your passport? Where is your luggage?) Let's look at how to form possessives in German.

Possessive adjectives

	Masc.	Fem.	Neuter	All plurals
my	mein	meine	mein	meine
your (*Sie*)	Ihr	Ihre	Ihr	Ihre
our	unser	unsere	unser	unsere
his/its	sein	seine	sein	seine
her	ihr	ihre	ihr	ihre
your (*du*)	dein	deine	dein	deine

When you want to indicate possession in German, you need to know the word that "matches" *who* is doing the possessing, and you need to know whether the object being possessed is masculine, feminine, neuter or plural. If I want to talk about *my* things, I need to use the word *mein* in German. *Das ist mein Mann.* (That is my husband.) *Hier ist mein Reisepaß.* (Here is my passport.) If I'm talking about things that are mine that are either feminine or plural, I need to add an *-e* ending to get *meine. Meine Tochter studiert in Kanada.* (My daughter studies in Canada.) *Wo sind meine Koffer?* (Where are my suitcases?)

The word for *your* (formal) is *Ihr*, and it follows the same ending rules as *mein*—add an *-e* if the possessed object is feminine or plural. *Ist das Ihr Mann? Hier ist Ihr Reisepaß. Studiert Ihre Tochter in Kanada? Wo sind Ihre Koffer?* You can see the other possessive adjectives in the table above—*unser* (our), *sein* (his/its), *ihr* (her), and *dein* (informal you). They all follow the same ending pattern.

If you have a masculine noun in the accusative case (where it is being "acted" on somehow and is "unequal" to the subject of the sentence—see p. 98), then you should change the ending on the possessive word to *-en*, just as *der* changes to *den* and *ein* changes to *einen* with a masculine noun in the accusative case. If we change *Hier ist Ihr Reisepaß* (an "equal-sign" type verb—*is*) to *Haben Sie Ihren Reisepaß?* (an "un-equal" type of verb—*have*), then we change *Ihr* to *Ihren*, so it is inflected for the accusative case.

Reality check: You are unlikely to want to use possessives beyond "my," so you may not want to invest the time in learning more about them. If you need to, you can look them up. And as for the accusative case, it's great if you have the time to learn those forms, but you can communicate quite well plowing merrily through your German using just nominative forms, however incorrect they might be.

Exercise 6.5
Which possessive adjective is correct in each answer?

1. Was macht Ihr Mann beruflich?
    Dein/Mein Mann ist Pilot.

2. Wo ist unser Gepäck?
    Ihr/Sein Gepäck ist hier.

3. Kommt seine Frau mit?
   Ja, seine/meine Frau kommt mit.

4. Was studiert dein Bruder?
   Mein/Dein Bruder studiert Mathematik.

5. Wie alt sind Ihre Kinder?
   Ihre/Unsere Kinder sind sieben und elf.

6. Wann fliegen ihre Elten nach Deutschland?
   Ihre/Unsere Eltern fliegen im Juli nach Deutschland.

7. Wie heißt seine Tochter?
   Seine/Unsere Tochter heißt Julia.

8. Wie ist Ihr Name?
   Dein/Mein Name ist Clark.

Answers: 1) Mein, 2) Ihr, 3) seine, 4) Mein, 5) Unsere, 6) Ihre, 7) Seine, 8) Mein

---

Culture note—Rain

German and Austrian weather can be very changeable. Sudden summer showers are common, as are all-day drizzles. It pays to carry a small umbrella whenever you go out.

Weather

weather	das Wetter	dahs *vet*-eh(r)
How is the weather?	Wie ist das Wetter?	vee ist dahs *vet-eh(r)?*
It's ___.	Es ist ___.	es ist ___
nice	schön	shern
bad	schlecht	shle^{ch}t
horrible	schrecklich	sh*Rek*-li^{ch}
cold	kalt	kahlt
cool	kühl	kewl
warm	warm	vah(r)m
hot	heiß	hice
clear	klar	klah(r)
sunny	sonnig	*zon*-i^{ch}

cloudy	wolkig	*vol-ki* [ch]
windy	windig	*vin-di* [ch]
foggy	neblig	*nay-bli* [ch]
It ___.	Es ___.	*es* ___
is snowing	schneit	*shnite*
is raining	regnet	*rayg-net*
is hailing	hagelt	*hah-gelt*
outside	draußen	*dRow-zen*

Exercise 6.6

What do you need to prepare yourself for the following weather conditions? Match the listings in columns A and B.

A

1. Es ist kühl.
2. Es regnet.
3. Es ist sonnig und windig.
4. Es schneit.
5. Es ist heiß und klar.

B

A. Badeanzug und Sonnenöl
B. Hut und Sonnenbrille
C. Jacke oder Pullover
D. Regenschirm
E. Mantel und Handschuhe

Answers: 1) C, 2) D, 3) B, 4) E, 5) A

Culture note—Hot weather

Germany and Austria can be quite cool in the summer, and in the past, heat waves were so limited that people endured them without fans or air conditioning. The climate has changed over the last several decades, though, with more extreme weather patterns.

Even though heat waves have grown more frequent and more intense, air conditioning and fans are still pretty rare. Some stores have air conditioning, and some restaurants, and some upper-end hotels, but homes don't and public places such as museums generally don't. I was surprised to find some air conditioning in Austria—some stores, some restaurants, and some upper-end hotels—but rarely ran across it in Germany.

Culture note—Celsius

Remember that Germany and Austria use the Celsius temperature scale. Water freezes at zero degrees Celsius and boils at 100 degrees. Twenty degrees Celsius is the quite pleasant temperature of 68 degrees Fahrenheit, while 32 degrees Celsius is a steamy 90 degrees Fahrenheit.

For a rough conversion of Celsius temperatures to Fahrenheit, double the Celsius number, then add 30. For example, start with 20 degrees Celsius, double it to 40, add 30 to get 70, which is close to the correct Fahrenheit reading of 68. This shortcut will usually not yield a perfectly accurate conversion, but it will at least get you in the ballpark.

Celsius reading x 2, + 30 =
approximate Fahrenheit reading

A final word

If you liked this book, please consider reviewing it on Amazon.com or barnesandnoble.com. And let's stay in touch! Follow me on Facebook at Elizabeth Bingham, Author. Join my email list for early book release information and occasional short newsletters at http://eepurl.com/bp3jtn. (Free Survival Summaries in German, Italian, and French when you sign up.)

Before you progress to the Self-Test, I'd like to ask you again to contact me about your experiences with this book and in Germany and Austria. Please tell me how things went, what worked and what didn't. Write me care of World Prospect Press, P.O. Box 253, Waverly, IA 50677 (www.worldprospect.com), or you can reach me via e-mail (bingham@worldprospect.com).

Have a great trip, and I look forward to hearing from you!

Appendix 1: Negation

You know the German word for "no": *nein*. Here are two other ways to indicate negation in German, the words for "not" and "no/none."

Nicht

Your "go-to" form of negation is the word "nicht," which means "not."

not	nicht	ni^{ch}t

I don't/won't take the bus.
Ich nehme den Bus <u>nicht</u>.

I'm not buying the shoes.
Ich kaufe die Schuhe <u>nicht</u>.

My wife is not here.
Meine Frau ist <u>nicht</u> hier.

The soup is not hot.
Die Suppe ist <u>nicht</u> heiß.

Kein/Keine

Another form of negation is needed, though, if you want to negate a noun that is preceded by a form of *ein/eine* or is not preceded by any article. Then you use a form of *kein/keine*.

not = no/none	kein/e	*kine/<u>ky</u>-neh*

Positive form: I drink wine. Ich trinke Wein.
or I drink <u>a</u> wine. Ich trinke <u>einen</u> Wein.

Negative form: I drink <u>no</u> wine. (= I don't drink wine.) Ich trinke <u>keinen</u> Wein.

Positive form: He is <u>an</u> American. Er ist Amerikaner.
Negative form: He is <u>not</u> an American. Er ist <u>kein</u> Amerikaner.

Positive form: We have time. Wir haben Zeit.
Negative form: We <u>don't</u> have time. Wir haben <u>keine</u> Zeit.

Positive form: I read <u>a</u> newspaper. Ich lese <u>eine</u> Zeitung.
Negative form: I <u>don't</u> read <u>a</u> newspaper. Ich lese <u>keine</u> Zeitung.

Contrast the two forms

Notice the difference in whether the definite article "the" is used or the indefinite article "an":

Positive form: I read <u>the</u> newspaper. Ich lese <u>die</u> Zeitung.
Negative form: I <u>don't</u> read <u>the</u> newspaper. Ich lese <u>die</u> Zeitung <u>nicht</u>.

Positive form: I read <u>a</u> newspaper. Ich lese <u>eine</u> Zeitung.
Negative form: I <u>don't</u> read <u>a</u> newspaper. Ich lese <u>keine</u> Zeitung.

Appendix 2: Technology

Internet	das Internet	*in-teh(r)-net*
wireless Internet	WLAN	*vay-lahn*
laptop	der Laptop	*lehp-top*
Internet café	das Internet Café	*in-teh(r)-net kah-fay*
access	der Zugang	*tsoo-gahng*
to connect	anschließen	*ahn-shlee-sen*
ready/done/ finished	fertig	*feh(r)-ti ᶜʰ*
e-mail address	die E-mail-Adresse	*ee-mayl-ah-dRess-eh*
to check	checken	*chek-en*
to log on	einloggen	*ine-log-en*
How do I log on?	Wie logge ich mich ein?	*vee log-eh i ᶜʰ mi ᶜʰ ine?*
password	das Passwort	*pahs-wohrt*
Are you on Facebook?	Sind Sie auf Facebook?	*zint zee owf fays-book?*
to download	herunterladen	*heh(r)-un-te(r)-lah-den*
printer	der Drucker	*dRuk-e(r)*
scanner	der Scanner	*skeh-ne(r)*
Skype	Skype	*skipe*
to use	benutzen	*beh-nuht-tsen*
headphones	der Kopfhörer	*kopf-heR-e(r)*
microphone	das Mikrofon	*mee-kRoh-fohn*
CD	die CD	*tsay-day*
to burn a CD	eine CD brennen	*ine-eh tsay-day bRen-en*
USB flash drive/memory stick	der USB-Stick	*oo-es-bay-stik*
crashed	abgestürzt	*ahp-geh-stew(r)tst*
fax number	die Faxnummer	*fahks-num-e(r)*

MP3 player	der MP3-Player	*em-pay-<u>dRy</u>-play-e(r)*
iPod	der iPod	*<u>eye</u>-pawd*
iPhone	der iPhone	*<u>eye</u>-fone*
cell phone	das Handy	*<u>hen</u>-dee*
prepaid cell phone	ein Handy mit Prepaidkarte	*ine <u>hen</u>-dee mit <u>pRee</u>-payd-kah(r)-teh*
SIM card	die SIM-Karte	*<u>zim</u>-kah(r)-teh*
cell number	die Handy-nummer	*<u>hen</u>-dee-num-e(r)*
charger	das Ladegerät	*<u>lah</u>-deh-geh-Rate*
network	das Netz	*nets*
phone card	die Telefonkarte	*teh-leh-<u>fohn</u>-kah(r)-teh*
international prepaid phone card	die internationale Prepaid-Telefonkarte	*in-te(r)-<u>naht</u>-see-oh-nah-lay <u>pree</u>-payd teh-leh-<u>fohn</u>-kah(r)-teh*
local phone call	das Ortsgespräch	*<u>oh(r)ts</u>-geh-spRech*
connection	die Verbindung	*feh(r)-<u>bin</u>-dung*
message (e.g., note)	die Nachtricht	*<u>nah</u>ch-Ri^{ch}t*
rates	die Gebühren	*geh-<u>bew</u>-Rehn*
cable	das Kabel	*<u>kah</u>-bel*
camera	die Kamera	*<u>kah</u>-meh-Rah*
digital camera	die Digital-kamera	*dig-ee-<u>tahl</u>-<u>kah</u>-meh-Rah*
disposable camera	die Wegwerf-kamera	*<u>vek</u>-ve(r)f- <u>kah</u>-meh-Rah*

German-English Dictionary

How to use this dictionary

The purpose of this dictionary is to help you decipher written and spoken German. Because you will be exposed to more German than you will need to produce, this dictionary contains more entries than the English-German dictionary that follows it. It is by no means comprehensive, however.

German words are listed in bold. Verbs are listed in the infinitive (*Sie*) form, as well as separate listings for some common inflected forms, especially irregular ones. Most nouns are listed in singular form, followed by *der, die* or *das* to indicate whether the noun is masculine, feminine or neuter, respectively. Plural forms of many nouns are noted in parentheses. Either add the indicated letters to the end of the word (for example: *Bohne, die (-n)* means the plural for bean is *Bohnen*) or change the part of the word that is repeated and pluralized in the parentheses (for example: *Bahnhof, der (-höfe)* means that the plural of train station is *Bahnhöfe*). If only a hyphen is listed in the parentheses, then the single and plural forms of the noun are the same (for example: *Enkel, der (-)* means that you don't need to change grandson to get grandsons). Pronunciations are not located here but are included in the English-German dictionary.

Aal, der (-e) eel
Abend, der evening
Abendbrot, das supper of open-faced sandwiches
Abendessen, das supper
abends p.m., in the evening
Abfahrt, die (-en) departure
Abfallkorb, der (-körber) trash can
abgestürzt crashed
acht eight
achtzehn eighteen
achtzig eighty
alkoholfrei non-alcoholic
allergisch allergic
Alphabet, das alphabet
Altstadt, die (-städte) old city

Amerika America, USA
Ananas, die (-se) pineapple
angekommen arrived
Ankunft, die (Ankünfte) arrivals
anprobieren to try on
anschließen to connect
Antazidum, das antacid
Antihistamin, das antihistamine
Apfel, der (Äpfel) apple
Apfelsaft, der apple juice
Apfelsine, die (-n) orange
Apfelstrudel, der apple tart

Apotheke, die (-n) pharmacy
Appetit, der appetite

Aprikose, die (-n) apricot
April April
arbeiten to work
Arbeiter/-in, der/die laborer, worker
arbeitslos unemployed
Architekt/-in, der/die architect
Arm, der (-e) arm
Armbanduhr, die (-en) wrist watch
Artischoke, die (-n) artichoke
Arzt, der (Ärzte) doctor (male)
Ärztin, die (-nen) doctor (female)
Asche, die (-n) ash
Aspirin, das aspirin
Aubergine, die (-n) eggplant
auch also
auf on, upon, up
aufpassen to pay attention
Aufschnitt, der cold cuts
Auf Wiederschauen goodbye
Auf Wiedersehen goodbye
Aufzug, der elevator
Auge, das (-n) eye
Augenoptiker, der optometrist
Augentropfen, die eye drops
August August
aus from
auschecken to check out
Ausfahrt, die (-en) road exit
Ausflug, der excursion
Ausgang, der (-gänge) exit
ausgebucht booked up, full
ausgesperrt locked out
Auskunft, die (-künfte) information
Ausland, das (-länder) foreign land
Australien Australia
Ausverkauf, der (-käufe) sale
Ausweis, der identification (card)
Auto, das (-s) car
Autohof, der (-höfe) highway rest
  stop
Baby, das (-s) baby
Babyflasche, die baby bottle
Babysitz, der baby seat
Back- fried
backen to bake
Bäckerei, die (-en) bakery
Bad, das (Bäder) bath
Badeanzug, der (-züge) bathing suit
Badehose, die (-en) bathing trunks

Badetuch, das large towel
Bahnhof, der (-höfe) train station
Bahnsteig, der (-e) platform
Banane, die (-n) banana
Bank, die (-en) bank
Bankomat, der ATM
Batterie, die (-n) battery
Bauer/Bäuerin, der/die farmer
Bauernschmaus, der hearty meat
  platter with sauerkraut
Bauernsuppe, die cabbage and
  sausage soup
Baum, der (Bäume) tree
Becher, der (-) cup, mug
Bedienung, die service
Bedienung inbegriffen service
  included
beginnen to begin
beige beige
Beilage, die (-n) accompaniment,
  side dish
Bein, das (-e) leg
benutzen to use
Benzin, das gasoline
Berg, der (-e) mountain
beruflich occupational(ly)
berühren to touch; Nicht berühren!
  Don't touch!
besetzt occupied
bestätigen to confirm
bestellen to order
Bettlaken, das sheet
bezahlen to pay
BH, der brassiere
Bier, das (-e) beer
Bierhalle, die (-n) beer hall
Bierkrug, der (-krüge) beer stein
Bierstube, die (-n) pub
billig cheap
billiger cheaper
bin, ich I am
Bio organic
Birne, die (-n) pear
bis to, until
bißchen, ein a little
bist, du you are (informal, singular)
bitte please (also "bitte bitte," "bitte
  schön")
blau blue
Blaukraut, das red cabbage

Blume, die (-n) flower
Blumenkohl, der cauliflower
Bluse, die (-n) blouse
Blutdruck, der blood pressure
blutig rare (meat)
Blutwurst, die (-würste) blood sausage
Bockbier, das a type of strong beer
Bockwurst, die (-würste) large frankfurter
Boden, der (Böden) floor
Bohne, die (-n) bean
Bonbon, der (-s) sweet (candy)
Boot, das (-e) boat
Bootsausflug, der boat trip
Bouillon, die clear soup
braten to roast
Bratkartoffeln, die fried potatoes
Bratwurst, die (-würste) bratwurst
brauchen to need
braun brown
brennen to burn
Brief, der (-e) letter
Briefkasten, der (-kästen) mailbox
Briefmarke, die (-n) postage stamp
Brille, die (-n) glasses
Brokkoli, der broccoli
Brot, das (-e) bread
Brötchen, das (-) roll
Brücke, die (-n) bridge
Bruder, der (Brüder) brother
Brust, die (Brüste) chest, breast
Brustkorb, der chest
Buch, das (Bücher) book
Buchhalter/-in, der/die accountant
Buchhandlung, die (-en) bookstore
Burg, die (-en) castle
Bus, der (-se) bus
Butter, die (no pl) butter
Café, das (-s) coffeehouse
checken to check
Cola, die (-s) cola
Cousin, der (-s) cousin (male)
Cousine, die (-n) cousin (female)
Currywurst, die sausage served in curry/ketchup sauce
da there
Dame, die (-n) lady

danke thank you (also "danke schön," "danke vielmals," "vielen Dank," and "herzlichen Dank")
dann then
das that, the (neut.)
Debitkarte, die debit card
Decke, die (-n) covering, ceiling; blanket
Deodorant, das (-s) deodorant
der the (masc.)
Deutsch German
Deutschland Germany
Dezember December
Diabetiker/-in, der/-in (-/-nen) diabetic person
die the (fem.)
Dienstag Tuesday
digital digital
Ding, das (-e) thing
Dom, der (-e) cathedral
Donnerstag Thursday
Doppelbock, das extra-strong bock beer
Doppelzimmer, das (-) double room
Dorsch, der cod
dort there
draußen outside
drei three
dreißig thirty
dreizehn thirteen
Drogerie, die (-n) drug store
drücken to press, to push
Drucker, der printer
du you (informal, singular)
dunkel dark
Dunkles, ein a dark beer
Durchfall, der diarrhea
durchgebraten, gut well-done (meat)
Dusche, die (-n) shower
Ei, das (-er) egg
Eierspeise, die (-n) egg dish
Einbahnstraße, die one-way street
einchecken to check in
einfach simple, one-way
Einfahrt, die (-en) road entrance
Eingang, der (-gänge) entrance
eingefroren frozen
einloggen to log on
eins one

Eintopf, der (-töpfe) stew
Eintritt, der (-e) entry, admittance
Eintrittskarte, die (-n) admission
   ticket
Einweg- disposable
Einzelzimmer, das (-) single room
Eis, das (no pl) ice, ice cream
Eisbein, das pig's knuckle
Eiscafé, das (-s) ice cream shop
Eisdiele, die (-n) ice cream shop
Eissalon, der (-s) ice cream shop
elf eleven
Eltern, die (no singular) parents
empfehlen to recommend
empfiehlst, du you recommend
empfiehlt, er/sie/es he/she/it
   recommends
enden to end
England England
englisch English; rare (meat)
Enkel, der (-) grandson
Enkel, die (-) grandchildren
Enkelin, die (-nen) granddaughter
Ente, die (-n) duck
Entschuldigen Sie Excuse me
Entschuldigung, die (-en) excuse
er he
Erbse, die (-n) pea
Erdapfel, der (-äpfel) potato (Austria)
Erdbeere, die (-n) strawberry
Erdgeschoß, das ground floor, first
   floor
Erdnuß, die (-nüsse) peanut
Erkältung, die (-en) cold (illness)
erlaubt allowed
Ermäßigung, die discount
Erwachsene, der/die (-n) adult
es it
essen to eat
Essig, der vinegar
etwas something
Euro, der unit of money for
   European Union
fahren to drive
Fahrkarte, die (-n) ticket
Fahrrad, das (-räder) bicycle
fährst, du you drive (informal,
   singular)
Fahrt, die (-en) trip, drive, ride
fährt, er/sie/es he/she/it drives

Familie, die (-n) family
Fasan, der (-e) pheasant
Februar February
Feder, die (-n) feather
Feld, das (-er) field
Fenster, das (-) window
Fensterplatz, der window seat
Ferienwohnung, die vacation
   apartment
fertig ready, finished, done
Festung, die (-en) fortress
Fett, das fat
feucht moist
feuchte Tücher wet wipes/baby
   wipes
Feuer, das (-) fire
Feuerwehr, die fire department
Fieber, das fever
Filetsteak, das (-s) beef steak
Film, der (-e) film
Finger, der (-) finger
Fisch, der (-e) fish
Fischgericht, das (-e) fish dish
Fitnessraum, der exercise room
FKK *Freikörperkultur,* nude beach
Flasche, die bottle
Flaschenöffner, der bottle opener
Fleisch, das (no pl) meat
Fleischgericht, das (-e) meat dish
Flug, der (Flüge) flight
Flughafen, der (-häfen) airport
Fluß, der (Flüsse) river
Forelle, die (-n) trout
Fotoapparat, der (-e) camera
Fotogeschäft, das (-e) photo shop
Fotographieren, das taking pictures
Frankfurter, die (-) hot dog
Frankreich France
Frau, die (-en) woman, wife
Fräulein, das (-) miss
frei vacant, available
Freitag Friday
Freund, der (-e) friend (male),
   boyfriend
Freundin, die (-nen) friend (female),
   girlfriend
Frikadelle, die (-n) meat patty
frisch fresh
Friseur, der (-e) hairdresser (male),
   barber

Friseuse, die (-n) hairdresser (female)
Frittatensuppe, die broth with
  pancake strips
früh early
Frühling, der spring
Frühstück, das breakfast
Führerschein, der (-e) driver's license
fünf five
fünfzehn fifteen
fünfzig fifty
für for
Fuß, der (Füße) foot
Gabel, die (-n) fork
Gans, die (Gänse) goose
Garderobe, die (-n) checkroom,
  cloakroom
Garnele, die (-n) shrimp
Garten, der (Gärten) garden, yard
Gas, mit with carbonation
Gasthaus, das (-häuser) restaurant,
  inn, hotel
Gaststätte, die (-n) restaurant
Gebäck, das pastries
gebacken baked
geblitzt "flashed" by a radar-
  triggered camera for a speeding
  ticket
gebraten fried, roasted
Gebühren, die rates
Geburtstag, der (-e) birthday
gedämpft steamed, stewed
Gefahr, die (-en) danger
Geflügel, das (no pl) fowl, poultry
gefüllt stuffed
gegen against, to
gegrillt grilled
gehackt diced
geheim secret
Geheimnummer, die PIN
gehen to go
Gehstock, der walking stick
Gewagen, der walker (walking frame)
gekocht boiled, cooked
gelb yellow
Geld, das money
Geldautomat, der ATM
Gelse, die (-n) mosquito (Austria)
gemischt mixed
Gemüse, das (-) vegetables
genug enough

geöffnet open
Gepäck, das (no pl) luggage
Gepäckaufbewahrung, die luggage
  checkroom
Gepäckschließfach, das luggage
  locker
geradeaus straight ahead
geräuchert smoked
Gericht, das (-e) dish (kind of food)
gern like to
Geröstete, die hash-browned
  potatoes
Geschäft, das (-e) store, shop
Geschäftsmann/-frau, der/die
  businessman/-woman
geschieden divorced
geschlossen closed
geschmort braised
geschwenkt sautéed
Geschwister, die (no singular) siblings
gestern yesterday
gestohlen stolen
gestorben deceased
gesund healthy
Gesundheit, die health
Getränk, das (-e) beverage, drink
Getreideflocken, die cereal
getrennt separate
getrocknet dried
Gewürz, das (-e) spice
Gibt es ____? Is there ____? Are
  there___?
Glas, das (Gläser) glass
Gleis, das (-e) train track
glücklich happy
golden gold, golden
Gott, der (Götter) God, god
Götterspeise, die like Jell-O
Grapefruitsaft, der grapefruit juice
Gras, das grass
grau gray
Grießnockerlsuppe, die soup with
  semolina dumplings
groß big
Großeltern, die (no singular)
  grandparents
Großmutter, die (-mütter)
  grandmother
Großvater, der (-väter) grandfather
grün green

grüßen to greet
Grüß Gott! Austrian greeting
Gugelhupf, der dry bundt cake
Gulasch, das goulash, spicy paprika and beef mixture
Gulaschsuppe, die goulash soup
günstig favorable, good, beneficial, reasonable
Gurke, die (-n) cucumber
gut good, well
gut durchgebraten well-done (meat)
gutbürgerliche Küche good plain cooking
haben to have
hageln to hail (weather)
Hahn, der (Hähne) rooster
Hähnchen, das (-) chicken
halb-durch medium (meat)
halbsüß semi-sweet (wine)
halbtrocken semi-sweet (wine)
Halloween, das Halloween
Hals, der neck, throat
Halt, der stop
halten to stop
Haltestelle, die (-n) bus/tram stop
Hammelfleisch, das mutton
Hand, die (Hände) hand
Handschuh, der (-e) glove
Handtasche, die (-n) purse
Handtuch, das small towel
Handy, das (-s) cell phone
Hase, der (-n) rabbit
Haselnuß, die (-nüsse) hazelnut
hast, du you have (informal, singular)
hat, er/sie/es he/she/it has
hatte, ich/er/sie/es I/he/she/it had
hatten, Sie/wir you (formal)/we had
hattest, du you had (informal, singular)
Hauptbahnhof, der (-höfe) main train station
Hauptgericht, das (-e) main course
Hauptplatz, der (-plätze) main square
Hausfrau, die (-en) housewife
hausgemacht homemade
Hausspezialität, die (-en) speciality of the house
Haustier, das (-e) pet

Haut, die skin
Heidelbeere, die (-n) blueberry
Heilbutt, der halibut
heiß hot
heiße, ich I am called
heißen to be called
heißt, er/sie/es/du he/she/it/you is/are called
Heizgerät, das heater
helfen to help
hell light
Helles, ein a light beer
Hemd, das (-en) shirt
Hendl, das (-) chicken
Herbst, der autumn, fall
Hering, der herring
Herr, der (-en) gentleman
Herr Ober! Waiter!
Herz, das (-en) heart
herunterladen to download
heuer this year (Austria)
heute today
hier here
Hilfe, die help
Himbeere, die (-n) raspberry
hin und zurück round trip, "there and back"
hoch high
Honig, der honey
Hose, die (-n) pair of pants
Hotel, das (-s) hotel
Hügel, der (-) hill
Huhn, das (Hühner) chicken
Hühnchen, das (-) chicken
Hühnerfleisch, das chicken
Hummer, der (-) lobster
Hund, der (-e) dog
hundert hundred
Hustenmittel, das (-) cough syrup
Hut, der (Hüte) hat
ich I
ihn him
Ihr you
im in
immer always
inbegriffen included (in price)
Informatiker/-in, der/die computer scientist
Ingenieur/-in, der/die engineer
inklusiv included

Inland, das home country, domestic
ißt, du/er/sie/es you/he/she/it
  eat(s)
ist, er/sie/es he/she/it is
Italien Italy
ja yes
Jacke, die (-n) jacket
Jahr, das (-e) year
Jänner January (Austria)
Januar January
Jeans, die jeans
Joghurt, der yogurt
Johannisbeere, die (-n) currant
Jugendherberge, die youth hostel
Juli July
Junge, der (-n) boy
Juni June
Kabel, das cable
Kaffee, der coffee, afternoon coffee
  time
Kaiserschmarren, der shredded
  pancake sprinkled with powdered
  sugar, often with raisins
Kalbfleisch, das veal
kalt cold
Kanada Canada
Kaninchen, das (-) rabbit
kann, ich/er/sie/es I/he/she/it
  can
kannst, du you can (informal,
  singular)
kaputt broken
Karaffe, die (-n) carafe
Karfiol, der cauliflower
Karotte, die (-n) carrot
Karpfen, der carp
Karte, die (-n) card, ticket
Kartoffel, die (-n) potato
Kartoffelbrei, der mashed potatoes
Kartoffelchips, die potato chips
Kartoffelklöße, die potato dumplings
Kartoffelkroketten, die potato
  croquettes
Kartoffelpuffer, die potato fritters
Käse, der cheese
Kasse, die cash register, box office
Kasseler Rippenspeer, der smoked
  pork chops
Katze, die (-n) cat

Kaufhaus, das (-häuser) department
  store
Kaugummi, der chewing gum
kein/keine no/none/not
Keks, der (-e) cookie, cracker
Ketchup, der ketchup
Keule, die (-n) leg, haunch
Kiefer, der (-) jaw
Kind, das (-er) child
Kinderbett, das child's bed
Kinderfahrkarte, die child's
  transportation ticket
Kinderkarte, die child's menu
Kinderportion, die (-en) child serving
Kindersitz, der child's seat
Kinderstuhl, der high chair
Kindertöpchen, das potty chair
Kinderwagen, der stroller
Kirche, die (-n) church
Kirsche, die (-n) cherry
klar clear
Kleid, das (-er) dress
Kleider, die clothes
klein small
Klempner/-in, der/die plumber
Klimaanlage, die air conditioning
Kloß, der (Klöße) dumpling
Klößchen, das (-) meatballs
Kneipe, die pub
Knie, das (-) knee
Knoblauch, der garlic
Knochen, der (-) bone
Knödel, der (-) dumpling
kochen to cook
koffeinfrei decaffeinated
Koffer, der (-) suitcase
Kohl, der cabbage
Kohlensäure, die carbonation, fizz
Kola, die (-s) cola
kommen to come
Konditorei, die (-en) pastry shop
können to be able to
Konto, das account (e.g., bank)
Kontrolle, die passport control
Kopf, der head
Kopfhörer, der headphones
Kopfkissen, das pillow
Kopfschmerzen, die headache
Kopfschmerztablette, die (-n)
  aspirin

Korkenzieher, der cork screw
kosten to cost
Kotelett, das (-s) chop, cutlet
Krabben, die shrimps
krank sick
Krankenhaus, das hospital
Krankenpfleger, der nurse (male)
Krankenschwester, die nurse
  (female)
Krankenwagen, der ambulance
Kraut, das cabbage
Krawatte, die (-n) necktie
Kreditkarte, die (-n) credit card
Kreisverkehr, der roundabout
Kren, der horseradish
Kuchen, der (-) cake
Krücke, die (-n) crutch
Kuckucksuhr, die (-en) cuckoo clock
Kugel, die (-n) sphere, scoop
kühl cool
Kühlschrank, der refrigerator
Kukuruz, der corn (Austria)
Kuli, der (-s) ballpoint pen
Künstler/-in, der/die artist
Lachs, der salmon
Ladegerät, das charger
Lammfleisch, das lamb meat
Lampe, die (-n) lamp, light fixture
Land, das (Länder) country
Landkarte, die (-n) map
lang long
langsam slow, slowly
Languste, die (-n) spiny lobster
Lauch, der (-e) leek
laufen to run
läufst, du you run (informal, singular)
läuft, er/sie/es he/she/it runs
laut loud
lauter louder, more loudly
Lebensgefahr, die danger to life
Leber, die liver
Leberkäse, der type of meatloaf
Leberknödelsuppe, die liver-
  dumpling soup
ledig single
Lehrer/-in, der/die teacher
leise quiet
Leiter/-in, der/die manager
Leitungswasser, das tap water
lesbisch lesbian

Licht, das (-er) light
Limonade, die (-n) soft drink
links left
Linsensuppe, die lentil soup
Liter, der (-) liter
Lob, das praise
Löffel, der (-) spoon
Luftpost, die airmail
Lunge, die (-n) lung
Mädchen, das (-) girl
Magen, der stomach
Magenschmerzen, die stomach
  pains
Mahlzeit! mid-day greeting, "Enjoy
  your meal" (Austria)
Mai May
Mais, der corn
Mandel, die (-n) almond, tonsil
Mann, der (Männer) man, husband
Mantel, der (Mäntel) coat, overcoat
Marille, die (-n) apricot (Austria)
mariniert marinated
Mark, die mark
Markt, der (Märkte) market
Marmelade, die (-n) jam
März March
Mass, die a liter of beer
Maut, die toll
Mayonnaise, die mayonnaise
Mechaniker/-in, der/die mechanic
Medikament, das (-e) medicine,
  medication
Meeresfrüchte, die seafood
Mehl, das flour
Mehlspeise, die dish with flour as
  the main ingredient, dessert
mehr more
Mehrwertsteuer, die sales tax
mein my
Menü, das (-s) set-priced meal or
  menu
Messe, die trade fair
Messer, das (-) knife
mieten to rent
Mietwagen, der (-) rental car
Milch, die milk
Milchprodukte, die dairy products
Million, die (-en) million
Mineralwasser, das mineral water
minus minus

Minute, die (-n) minute
mit with
Mitnehmen, zum take out, to take away
Mittag, der noon
Mittagessen, das lunch
Mitte, die middle
mittel medium (meat)
Mitternacht, die midnight
Mittwoch Wednesday
möbliert furnished
möchten would like to
Mohrrübe, die (-n) carrot
Moment, der moment
Monat, der (-e) month
Montag Monday
morgen tomorrow
Morgen, der early morning
morgens in the morning
Motorrad, das (-räder) motorcycle
Mücke, die (-n) mosquito
müde tired
Mund, der mouth
Muscheln, die mussels
Museum, das (Museen) museum
Musiker/-in, der/die musician
Muskel, der (-n) muscle
Mutter, die (Mütter) mother
Muttermilchersatz, der baby formula
Muttertag, der Mother's Day
nach after (time), to (destination)
Nachmittag, der afternoon
Nachspeise, die (-n) dessert
Nacht, die (Nächte) night
Nachtisch, der (-e) dessert
Nachtricht, die message (e.g., note)
Nähe, in der nearby
Name, der (-n) name
Nase, die nose
Nasenspray, das nose spray
Nasentropfen, die nose drops
Navigationssystem, das GPS navigator
Navi-System, das GPS navigator
neb(e)lig foggy
Neffe, der (-n) nephew
nehmen to take
nein no
Netz, das network

neun nine
neunzehn nineteen
neunzig ninety
nicht not
Nichte, die (-n) niece
Nieren, die kidneys
Nonne, die (-n) nun
nördlich to the north
November November
Nudel, die (-n) noodle
null zero
nur only
Nuß, die (Nüsse) nut
Ober!, Herr Waiter!
Obers, das whipped cream
Obst, das fruit
Ochsenschwanzsuppe, die oxtail soup
oder or
ohne without
Ohr, das (-en) ear
Oktober October
Öl, das oil
Oma, die (-s) grandma
Omelett, das (-e) omelette
Onkel, der (-) uncle
Opa, der (-s) grandpa
orange orange
Orange, die (-n) orange
Ortsgespräch, das local phone call
Österreich Austria
östlich to the east
Paket, das package, parcel
Palast, der (Paläste) palace
Palatschinken, die thin rolled pancake with sweet filling
paniert breaded
Papier, das (-e) paper
Papierkorb, der waste basket
Paradeiser, der (-) tomato (Austria)
Pardon! pardon me
Park, der (-e) park
Parkverbot no parking
Partner/-in, der/die (-/-nen) partner
Paß, der (Pässe) passport
Paß auf! Passen Sie auf! Pay attention! Watch out!
Passwort, das password
Pellkartoffel, die (-n) baked potato in skin

Penizillin, das penicillin
Pension, die (-en) guesthouse, B&B
per by
Person, die (-en) person
Petersilienkartoffeln, die parsley
　potatoes
Pfand, das (Pfänder) deposit
Pfarrer/-in, der/die minister
Pfeffer, der pepper
Pfennig, der (-e) penny
Pfirsich, der (-e) peach
Pflanze, die (-n) plant
Pilot/-in, der/die pilot
Pils, das Pilsner beer
Pilz, der (-e) mushroom
Platz am Gang aisle seat
Plätzchen, das (-) cookie
Polizei, die police
Pommes frites, die French fries
Portion, die (-en) portion
Post, die mail, post office
Postkarte, die (-n) postcard
Postleitzahl, die zip code
Preiselbeere, die (-n) cranberry
preisgünstig low-cost, economical
prickelnd sparkling
Priester, der priest
Professor/-in, der/die professor
Prost! Cheers!
Pullover, der (-) pullover, sweater
-püree creamed
Puter, der turkey (Austria)
Quittung, die (-en) receipt
Rad, das (Räder) wheel, bike
Radler, der light beer with lemonade
Rahm, der cream
Rasierapparat, der electric razor
Rasiercreme, die shaving cream
Rasierklinge, die razor blade
Rasiermesser, das razor blade
Rasthof, der rest stop
Raststation, die (-en) rest stop
Rathaus, das (-häuser) town hall
Rauchen, das smoking
Räucher- smoked-
rechts right
Rechtsanwalt/anwältin, der/die
　lawyer
Rechnung, die bill
recyceln to recycle

Regenschirm, der (-e) umbrella
regnen to rain
Reh, das (-e) deer
Reifen, der (-) tire
Reifepanne, die flat tire
Reis, der rice
Reisescheck, der (-s) traveler's check
Reißverschluss, der zipper, traffic
　merge
Rentner/-in, der/die retired person
reparieren to fix/repair
Reservierung, die (-en) reservation
Restaurant, das (-s) restaurant
Restmüll, der non-recyclable waste
Rezept, das (-e) prescription
Rindfleisch, das beef
Rock, der (Röcke) skirt
roh raw
Rohschinken, der cured ham
Roller, der (-) scooter
Rollladen, der (-läden) exterior roll-
　up shutters on windows
Rollstuhl, der wheelchair
rosa pink
Rosenkohl, der Brussels sprouts
Rost, vom grilled, broiled
Rostbraten, der rump steak
Rösti, die hash-browned potatoes
rot red
Rotkohl, der red cabbage
Rotwein, der red wine
Roulade, die (-n) meat roll
Rücken, der back
rufen to call
Ruhetag, der day of rest, closed for
　the day
Rühreier, die scrambled eggs
Saft, der (Säfte) juice
Sahne, die cream
Salat, der (-e) salad
Salz, das salt
salzig salty
Salzkartoffeln, die boiled potatoes
Samstag Saturday
Sardellen, die anchovies
Sardinen, die sardines
sauber clean
sauer sour
Sauerbraten, der braised beef
　marinated in vinegar and herbs

SB abbreviation for self-service
S-Bahn, die (-en) city/suburban train
Schaltiere, die shellfish
schauen to look
Scheibe, die slice
Schilling, der schilling
Schinken, der ham
schlafen to sleep
Schlafsack, der sleeping bag
schläfst, du you sleep (informal, singular)
schläft, er/sie/es he/she/it sleeps
Schlagobers, das whipped cream
Schlagrahm, der whipped cream
Schlagsahne, die whipped cream
schlecht bad
Schließfach, das (-fächer) locker
Schlips, der (-e) necktie
Schloß, das (Schlösser) palace, castle
Schlüssel, der (-) key
schmecken to taste
schmeckt gut, es it tastes good
schmutzig dirty
Schnecke, die (-n) snail
schneien to snow
Schnellimbiß, der (-imbisse) snack bar
Schnitzel, das schnitzel, escalope
Schnuller, der pacifier
Schokolade, die (-n) chocolate
schön pretty, nice
schrecklich terrible
Schreibpapier, das writing paper
Schriftsteller/-in, der/die writer
Schrippe, die (-n) roll (Berlin)
Schuh, der (-e) shoe
Schulter, die (-n) shoulder
schwach weak
schwanger pregnant
schwarz black
Schweinefleisch, das pork
Schweinekotelett, das (-s) pork chop
Schweiz, die Switzerland
Schwester, die (-n) sister
Schwimmbad, das swimming pool
Schwimmweste, die life jacket
schwul gay, homosexual
sechs six
sechzehn sixteen
sechzig sixty

See, der (-n) lake
See, die (-n) sea
seekrank seasick
Seezunge, die sole
Seife, die (-n) soap
sein to be
Sekretär/-in, der/die secretary
Sekt, der champagne
Sekunde, die (-n) second
Selbständige, der/die self-employed person
Selbstbedienung, die self-service
Semmel, die (-n) roll (Austria)
Senf, der mustard
September September
Serviette, die (-n) napkin
Servus! Austrian greeting, goodbye
Shampoo, das (-s) shampoo
Sie you (formal)
sie her
sieben seven
siebzehn seventeen
siebzig seventy
silbern silver
sind, Sie you are (formal)
sind, wir we are
Socke, die (-n) sock
Sohn, der (Söhne) son
Sommer, der summer
Sonderangebot, das special offer
Sonnabend Saturday
Sonnenbrille, die (-n) sunglasses
Sonnencreme, die suntan lotion
Sonnenöl, das suntan oil
sonnig sunny
Sonntag Sunday
Spanferkel, das (-) suckling pig
Spanien Spain
Spargel, der asparagus
Sparkasse, die (-n) savings bank
spät late
Spätzle, die kind of small noodle, like tiny gnocchi
Speck, der bacon
Speicherkarte, die (-n) memory card
Speisekarte, die (-n) menu
Spezialität des Hauses, die (-en) specialty of the house
Spiegelei, das (-er) fried egg
Spielplatz, der playground

Spielzeug, das toy
spreche, ich I speak
sprechen to speak
sprichst, du you speak (informal, singular)
spricht, er/sie/es he/she/it speaks
sprudelnd sparkling
Stadt, die (Städte) city
Stadtmitte, die city center
Stadtplan, der (-pläne) city map
Stammtisch, der regulars' table
Stau, der traffic jam
still non-carbonated
stören to disturb
Straßenbahn, die (-en) streetcar
Streichkäse, der cheese spread
Strom, der electricity
Stück, das (-e) piece
Student/-in, der/die student
Stuhl, der (Stühle) chair
Stunde, die (-n) hour
Stundenhotel, das hourly-rate hotel
suchen to look for
südlich to the south
Supermarkt, der (-märkte) supermarket
Suppe, die (-n) soup
süß sweet
Süßigkeit, das (-en) sweet, candy
Süßspeise, die (-n) dessert
Süßstoff, der artificial sweetener
Tabakhändler, der tobacconist's shop
Tabakhandlung, die tobacconist's shop
Tabaktrafik, die tobacconist's shop (Austria)
Tag, der (-e) day
Tagesausflug, der day trip
Tageskarte, di day ticket
Tagesmenü, das set menu of day
Tagessuppe, die soup of the day
Tankstelle, die (-n) gas station
Tante, die (-n) aunt
Taschenlampe, die flashlight
Taschentuch, das (-tücher) facial tissue
tausend thousand
Taxi, das (-s) cab, taxi
Tee, der tea

Teich, der (-e) pond
Teigwaren, die pasta
Telefon, das (-e) telephone
Teller, der (-) plate
teuer expensive
Thunfisch, der tuna
Tier, das animal
Tisch, der (-e) table
Tischler, der carpenter
Toast, der toast
Tochter, die (Töchter) daughter
Toilette, die (-n) toilet, bathroom
Toilettenpapier, das toilet paper
Tomate, die (-n) tomato
Tomatenketchup, der ketchup
Torte, die (-n) fancy cake, layer cake
Touristeninformation, die tourist information
Traube, die (-n) grape
traurig sad
trinken to drink
trocken dry
Trockner, der dryer
Truthahn, der turkey
tschüs 'bye
T-Shirt, das (-s) T-shirt
tun to do
Tür, die (-en) door
Tüte, die bag, sack
U-Bahn, die (-en) subway
über over
überbacken oven-browned
überzogen overdrawn
Uhr, die (-en) clock, o'clock
Umschlag, der envelope
umsteigen to change (e.g., trains)
und and
Unfal, der accident
unten under, down
Unterhose, die (-n) pair of underwear, brief, panty
unterschreiben to sign
Unterwäsche, die underclothes
USA, die the USA
USB-Stick, der flash drive
Valentinstag, der Valentine's Day
Vater, der (Väter) father
Vatertag, der Father's Day
Verbindung, die connection
verboten forbidden

Vereinigten Staaten, die the United
  States
verheiratet married
Verkäufer/-in, der/die salesperson
verloren lost
Verpackung, die packaging
Verschreibung, die (-en)
  prescription
Versicherung, die insurance
verspätet delayed
Verspätung, die delay
verstehen to understand
Verstopfung, die constipation
Vertreter/-in, der/die sales
  representative
verwitwet widowed
Verzeihung, Verzeihen Sie Pardon
  me! Excuse me!
verzollen to declare (at a border
  crossing)
Vetter, der (-n) male cousin
viel much
vier four
Viertel, der quarter
vierzehn fourteen
vierzig forty
Vignette, die traffic toll sticker
violett purple
Vogel, der bird
volltanken to fill the tank up
von. . . bis from. . . to
vor before
Vormittag, der mid- and late
  morning
Vorsicht, die caution, Look out!
Vorspeise, die (-n) appetizer
Wagen, der (-) car
Wand, die (Wände) wall
wann when
war, ich/er/sie/es I/he/she/it was
waren, Sie/wir you were (formal),
  we were
warm warm
warst, du you were (informal,
  singular)
warum why
was what
Wasser, das water
Wassermelone, die (-n) watermelon
WC, das water closet, toilet

wechseln to exchange
Wechselstube, die currency
  exchange office
weg away
Wegwerf- disposable
weh hurt
Weihnachten, die Christmastime
Wein, der (-e) wine
Weinliste, die wine list
Weintraube, die (-n) grape
weiß white
Weißbier, das white beer, made from
  wheat
Weißwein, der white wine
weit far
wenig little
weniger fewer, less
wer who
westlich to the west
Wetter, das weather
Wickelraum, der baby-changing
  room
wie how
wiederholen to repeat
Wiederschauen! goodbye
Wiedersehen! goodbye
wie lange how long
Wiener Schnitzel, der Wiener
  schnitzel
Wiener Würstchen, das (-) hot dog
Wiese, die (-n) meadow
wieviel how much
wie viele how many
wild wild, game
Wildschwein, das (-e) wild boar
Windel, die (-n) diaper
windig windy
Winter, der winter
wir we
Wissenschaftler/-in, der/die
  scientist
WLAN wireless Internet
wo where
Woche, die (-n) week
Wochenende, das (-n) weekend
Wochenkarte, die week ticket
woher where from
wohin where to
wolkig cloudy
Wurst, die (Würste) sausage

Würstel, das (-)   sausage (Austria)
Würstelstand, der (-stände) sausage
    stand
Würze, die   seasoning
zäh   tough
Zahl, die (-en)   number
Zahlen!   Check, please!
Zahn, der (Zähne)   tooth
Zahnarzt/-in, der/die   dentist
Zahnpasta, die   toothpaste
zehn   ten
Zeit, die   time
Zeitschrift, die (-en)   magazine
Zeitung, die (-en)   newspaper
Zelt, das   tent
zelten   to camp
Zentrum, das   center
zerbrechlich   fragile
ziehen   to pull
Zigarette, die (-n)   cigarette
Zigarre, die (-n)   cigar
Zimmer, das (-)   room
Zimmermann, der   carpenter
Zitrone, die (-n)   lemon
Zoll, der   toll, customs
Zollerklärung, die   customs
    declaration
zu   to, too
Zucker, der   sugar
Zug, der (Züge)   train
Zugang, der   access
Zum Wohl!   To your health!
Zunge, die   tongue
zurück   back
zusammen   together
Zutritt, Kein   No Entry
zwanzig   twenty
zwei   two
Zwiebel, die (-n)   onion
Zwiebelsuppe, die   onion soup
zwischen   between
zwo   two
zwölf   twelve

English-German Dictionary

How to use this dictionary

English words are listed in bold. Most German verbs are listed in infinitive form; you will need to change them to get the *ich* form. Most nouns are listed in singular. If you need plural forms, look up the German word in the German-English dictionary.

able to, to be können [ker-nen]
access Zugang, der [tsoo-gahng]
accident Unfall, der [oon-fahl]
account (e.g., bank) Konto, das [kon-toh]
accountant Buchhalter/-in, der/die [booch-hahl-teh(r)/-in]
admittance Eintritt, der [ine-tRit]
admittance ticket Eintrittskarte, die [ine-tRits-kah(r)-teh]
adult Erwachsene, der/die, [eh(r)-vah^ch^-seh-neh]
after nach [nahch]
afternoon Nachmittag, der [nahch-mit-ahk]
against gegen [gay-gen]
air conditioning Klimaanlage, die [klee-mah-ahn-lah-geh]
airmail Luftpost, die [luft-post]
airport Flughafen, der [flook-hah-fen]
aisle seat Platz am Gang, der [plahts ahm gahng]
alcohol-free beer alkoholfreies Bier [ahl-koh-hohl-fRy-es bee(r)]
allergic allergisch [ah-leh(r)-gish] (**to** gegen [gay-gen])
allowed erlaubt [eh(r)-lowpt]
almond Mandel, die [mahn-del]
alphabet Alphabet, das [ahl-fah-bet]
also auch [owch]
always immer [im-eh(r)]
am, I ich bin [i^ch^ bin]
ambulance Krankenwagen, der [kRank-en-vah-gen]
America Amerika [ah-may-Ree-kah]
and und [unt]
animal Tier, das [tee(r)]

antacid Antazidum, das [ahn-tah-tsee-dum]
antihistamine Antihistamin, das [ahn-tee-hist-ah-meen]
appetite Appetit, der [ah-peh-teet]
appetizer Vorspeise, die [foh(r)-shpy-zeh]
apple Apfel, der [ahp-fel]
apple juice Apfelsaft, der [ahp-fel-zaft]
apple tart Apfelstrudel, der [ahp-fel-shtRoo-del]
apricot Aprikose, die [ah-pRee-koh-zeh]; Marille, die [mah-Ril-eh] (Aust.)
April April [ah-pRil]
architect Architekt/-in, der/die [ah(r)-^ch^ee-tekt/-in]
are, there es gibt [es geept]
Are there ___? Gipt es ___? [geept es ___?]
are, you Sie sind [zee zint] (formal); du bist [doo bist] (informal, singular)
arm Arm, der [ah(r)m]
arrivals Ankunft , die [ahn-kunft]
arrived angekommen [ahn-geh-kom-en]
artificial sweetener Süßstoff, der [zews-shtof]
artist Künstler/-in, der/die [kewnst-leh(r)/-in]
ash Asche, die [ah-sheh]
asparagus Spargel, der [shpah(r)-gehl]
aspirin Aspirin, das [ah-spee-Reen]; Kopfschmerztablette, die [kopf-shmeh(r)ts-tah-blet-eh]
ATM Geldautomat, der [gelt-ow-toh-maht]; Bankomat, der [bahnk-oh-maht]

August August [ow-_gust_]
aunt Tante, die [_tahn_-teh]
Australia Australien [ow-_strahl_-yen]
Austria Österreich [_er_-steh(r)-Ry^{ch}]
autumn Herbst, der [heh(r)pst]
available frei [fRy]
away weg [veck]
baby Baby, das [_bay_-bee]
baby bottle Babyflasche, die [_bay_-
bee-_flah_-sheh]
baby-changing room Wickelraum,
der [_vik_-el-Rowm]
baby formula Muttermilchersatz, der
[_mut_-e(r)-mil^{ch}-e(r)-zahts]
baby seat Babysitz, der [_bay_-bee-zits]
babysitter Babysitter, der [_bay_-bee-
sit-e(r)]
baby wipes feuchte Tücher [foy$_{ch}$-
teh tew^{ch}-e(r)]
back (body part) Rücken, der [_Rew_-
ken]; (direction) zurück [tsoo-_Rewk_]
bacon Speck, der [shpeck]
bad schlecht [shle^{ch}t]
bag Tüte, die [_tew_-teh]
bakery Bäckerei, die [bek-eh-_Rye_]
banana Banane, die [bah-_nah_-neh]
B and B Pension, die [pen-_zyohn_]
bank Bank, die [bahnk]; Sparkasse,
die [_shpah(r)_-kah-seh]
barber Friseur, der [fRi-_zew(r)_]
bath Bad, das [baht]
bathing suit Badeanzug, der [_bah_-
deh-ahn-tsook]
bathing trunks Badehose, die [_bah_-
deh-hoh-zeh]
bathroom Toilette, die [toy-_let_-eh]
battery Batterie, die [bah-teh-_Ree_]
be, to sein [zine]
bean Bohne, die [_boh_-neh]
beef Rindfleisch, das [_Rint_-flysh]
beer Bier, das [bee(r)]
beer hall Bierhalle, die [_bee(r)_-hahl-eh]
beer/lemonade mixture Radler, der
[_Raht_-leh(r)]
beer, liter of Maß, die [mahs]
beer, non-alcoholic alkoholfreies
Bier [ahl-koh-hohl-_fRy_-es bee(r)]
beer stein Bierkrug, der [_bee(r)_-kRuk]
before vor [foh(r)]
begin, to beginnen [beh-_gin_-en]
beige beige [bayzh]

beneficial günstig [_gewn_-sti^{ch}]
between zwischen [_tsvish_-en]
bicycle Rad, das [Raht]; Fahrrad, das_
[_fah(r)_-Raht]
big groß [gRohs]
bike Rad, das [Raht]; Fahrrad, das_
[_fah(r)_-Raht]
bill Rechnung, die [_Re^{ch}_-nung]
bird Vogel, der [_foh_-gehl]
birthday Geburtstag, der [geh-
boo(r)ts-tahk]
black schwarz [shvah(r)ts]
blanket Decke, die [_dek_-eh]
blood pressure Blutdruck, der [_bloot_-
dRuk]
blood sausage Blutwurst, die [_bloot_-
vu(r)st]
blouse Bluse, die [_bloo_-zeh]
blue blau [blau]
blueberry Heidelbeere, die [_hy_-del-
bay-Reh]
boat Boot, das [boht]
boat excursion Bootsausflug, der
[_bohts_-ows-flook]
boiled gekocht [geh-_ko$_{ch}$t_]
bone Knochen, der [_kno$_{ch}$_-en]
book Buch, das [boo$_{ch}$]
bookstore Buchhandlung, die [_boo$_{ch}$_-
hant-lung]
bottle opener Flaschenöffner, der
[_flah_-shen-_erf_-neh(r)]
box office Kasse, die [_kah_-seh]
boy Junge, der [_yung_-eh]
boyfriend Freund, der [fRoynt]
brassiere BH, der [bay-hah]
bratwurst Bratwurst, die [_bRaht_-
vu(r)st]
bread Brot, das [bRoht]
breakfast Frühstück, das [_fRew_-stewk]
breast Brust, die [bRust]
bridge Brücke, die [_bRew_-keh]
bright hell [hel]
broccoli Brokkoli, der [_bRok_-ol-ee]
broken kaputt [kah-_put_]
brother Bruder, der [_bRoo_-deh(r)]
brown braun [bRown]
bus Bus, der [bus]
businessman/-woman
Geschäftsmann/-frau, der/die [geh-
shefts-mahn/-fRow]

bus stop Haltestelle, die [hal-teh-shtel-eh]

butter Butter, die [but-eh(r)]

by (via) per [pe(r)]; (next to) neben [nay-ben]

'bye tschüs [chews]; servus [zeh(r)-voos]

cab Taxi, das [tahk-see]

cabbage Kraut, das [kRowt]; Kohl, der [kohl]

cable Kabel, das [kah-bel]

cake Kuchen, der [koo-ᴄₕen]

cake, fancy Torte, die [to(r)-teh]

call, to rufen [Roo-fen]

called, to be heißen [hy-sen]

camera Fotoapparat, der [foh-toh-ah-pah-Rat]; Kamera, die [kah-meh-Rah]

camera, digital Digital-kamera, die [dig-ee-tahl-kah-meh-Rah]

camera, disposable Wegwerf-kamera, die [vek-ve(r)f- kah-meh-Rah]

camera shop Fotogeschäft, das [foh-toh-geh-sheft]

camp, to zelten [tselt-en]

Canada Kanada [kah-nah-dah]

candy Bonbon, der [bon-bon]

car Auto, das [ow-toh]; Wagen, der [vah-gen]

carafe Karaffe, die [kay-Rah-feh]

carbonated mit Kohlensäure [mit koh-len-zoy-Reh]

carbonated, non- still [shtil]

carbonation Kohlensäure, die [koh-len-zoy-Reh]

card Karte, die [kah(r)-teh]

carpenter (buildings) Zimmermann, der [tsim-eh(r)-mahn]; (furniture) Tischler/-in, der/die [tish-leh(r)/-in]

carrot Karotte, die [kah-Rot-eh]; Mohrrübe, die [moh(r)-Rew-beh]

cash register Kasse, die [kah-seh]

castle Burg, die [boo(r)k]; Schloß, das [shlos]

cat Katze, die [kaht-seh]

cathedral Dom, der [dohm]

cauliflower Blumenkohl, der [bloo-men-kohl] ; Karfiol, der [kah(r)-fee-ohl] (Aust.)

caution Vorsicht, die [foh(r)-ziᶜʰt]

CD CD, die [tsay-day]

CD, to burn a eine CD brennen [ine-eh tsay-day bRen-en]

ceiling Decke, die [dek-eh]

cell number Handynummer, die [hen-dee-num-e(r)]

cell phone Handy, das [hen-dee]

center Zentrum, das [tsen-tRum]

cereal Getreideflocken, die [geh-tRy-deh-flok-en]

chair Stuhl, der [shtool]

champagne Sekt, der [zekt]

change, to (e.g., trains) umsteigen [oom-shtyg-en]

charger (tech.) Ladegerät, das [lah-deh-geh-Rate]

cheap billig [bil-iᶜʰ]

cheaper billiger [bil-iᶜʰ-eh(r)]

Check, please! 'Zahlen, bitte! [tsahl-en, bit-eh]

check, to checken [chek-en]

check in, to einchecken [ine-chek-en]

check out, to auschecken [ows-chek-en]

checkroom Garderobe, die [gah(r)-deh-Roh-beh]

Cheers! Prost! [pRohst]

cheese Käse, der [kay-zeh]

cheese spread Streichkäse, der [shtRyᶜʰ-kay-zeh]

cherry Kirsche, die [ki(r)-sheh]

chest Brustkorb, der [bRust-ko(r)p]; Brust, die [bRust]

chewing gum Kaugummi, der [kow-gum-ee]

chicken Hähnchen, das [hen-ᶜʰen]; Huhn, das [hoon]; Hühnchen, das [hewn-ᶜʰen]; Hühnerfleisch, das [hewn-eh(r)-flysh]

child Kind, das [kint]

child's bed Kinderbett, das [kin-deh(r)-bet]

child serving/portion Kinderportion, die [kin-deh(r)-po(r)-tsyohn]

child's menu Kinderkarte, die [kin-deh(r)-kah(r)-teh]

child's seat Kindersitz, der [kin-deh(r)-zits]

child's ticket (transportation) Kinderfahrkarte, die [kin-deh(r)-fah(r)-kah(r)-teh]

chocolate Schokolade, die [sho-ko-lah-deh]

Christmastime Weihnachten [vy-na$_{ch}$-ten]

church Kirche, die [ki(r)-^{ch}eh]

cigar Zigarre, die [tsi-gah(r)-eh]

cigarette Zigarette, die [tsig-ah-Ret-eh]

city Stadt, die [shtaht]

city center Stadtmitte, die [shtaht-mit-eh]

city map Stadtplan, der [shtaht-plahn]

clean sauber [zow-beh(r)]

clear klar [klah(r)]

cloakroom Garderobe, die [gah(r)-deh-Roh-beh]

clock Uhr, die [oo(r)]

closed geschlossen [geh-shlos-en]

closing day Ruhetag, der [Roo-eh-tahk]

clothes Kleider, die [kly-deh(r)]

cloudy wolkig [vol-ki^{ch}]

coat Mantel, der [mahn-tel]

coffee Kaffee, der [kah-fay] (Germ.); Kaffee, der [kah-fay] (Aust.)

coffeehouse Café, das [kah-fay]

cola Cola, die [koh-lah]

cold (temp.) kalt [kahlt]; (illness) Erkältung, die [eh(r)-kel-tung]

cold cuts Aufschnitt, der [owf-schnit]

come, to kommen [kom-en]

computer scientist Informatiker/-in, der/die [in-fo(r)-mah-tik-eh(r)/-in]

conference Konferenz, die [kon-feh-Rents]

confirm, to bestätigen [beh-shtay-teeg-en]

connect, to (tech.) anschließen [ahn-shlee-sen]

connection Verbindung, die [feh(r)-bin-dung]

constipation Verstopfung, die [feh(r)-shtop-fung]

cook, to kochen [ko$_{ch}$-en]

cooked gekocht [geh-ko$_{ch}$t]

cookie Keks, der [kayks]

cool kühl [kewl]

cork screw Korkenzieher, der [koh(r)-ken-tsee-e(r)]

corn Mais, der [mice]

cost, to kosten [kos-ten]

cough syrup Hustenmittel, das [hoos-ten-mit-el]

country Land, das [lahnt]

cousin (female) Cousine, die [koo-zee-neh]; (male) Cousin, der [ku-zeng]

covering Decke, die [dek-eh]

cracker Keks, der [kayks]

crashed (tech.) abgestürzt [ahp-geh-stew(r)tst]

cream Sahne, die [zah-neh]; Rahm, der [Rahm]

cream, whipped Schlagsahne, die [shlahk-zah-neh]; Schlagobers, das [shlahk-oh-beh(r)s]; Schlagrahm, der [shlahk-Rahm]

credit card Kreditkarte, die [kReh-deet-kah(r)-teh]

crutch Krücke, die [kRew-keh]

cuckoo clock Kuckucksuhr, die [koo-kooks-oo(r)]

cup Tasse, die [tah-seh]; Becher, der [be^{ch}-eh(r)]

currency exchange office Wechselstube, die [ve^{ch}-sel-shtoo-beh]

customs (toll/duty) Zoll, der [tsol]

customs declaration Zoll-erklärung, die [tsol-eh(r)-klehR-ung]

daily special (meal) Tagesmenü, das [tahg-es-meh-new]

damaged beschädigt [beh-shay-digt]

danger Gefahr, die [geh-fah(r)]

dangerous gefährlich [geh-feh(r)-li^{ch}]

danger to life Lebensgefahr, die [lay-bens-geh-fah(r)]

dark dunkel [dunk-el]

dark beer, a ein Dunkles [ine dunk-les]

daughter Tochter, die [to$_{ch}$-teh(r)]

day Tag, der [tahk]

day of rest Ruhetag, der [Roo-eh-tahk]

day ticket Tageskarte, die [tahg-es-kah(r)-teh]

day trip Tagesausflug, der [tahg-es-ows-flook]

debit card Debitkarte, die [day-bit-kah(r)-teh]

decaffeinated koffeinfrei [kof-eh-een-fRy]

deceased gestorben [geh-shto(r)-ben]

December Dezember [deh-tsem-be(r)]

declare, to (at border crossing) verzollen [feh(r)-tsol-en]

declare, I have nothing to Ich habe nichts zu verzollen. [i^{ch} hah-beh ni^{ch}ts tsoo feh(r)-tsol-en]

declare, I have something to Ich habe etwas zu verzollen. [i^{ch} hah-beh et-vahs tsoo feh(r)-tsol-en]

deer Reh, das [Ray]

delay Verspätung, die [feh(r)-shpay-tung]

delayed verspätet [feh(r)-shpay-tet]

dentist Zahnarzt/-ärztin, der/die [tsahn-ah(r)tst/eh(r)t-stin]

deodorant Deodorant, das [day-oh-doh-Rahnt]

department store Kaufhaus, das [kowf-hows]

departure Abfahrt, die [ahp-fah(r)t]

deposit Pfand, das [pfahnt]

dessert Nachspeise, die [na_{ch}-shpy-zeh]; Nachtisch, der [nah_{ch}-tish]

diabetic Diabetiker/-in, der/die [dee-ah-beh-tee-keh(r)/-in]

diaper Windel, die [vin-del]

diarrhea Durchfall, der [du(r)_{ch}-fahl]

digital digital [dig-i-tahl]

digital camera Digital-kamera, die [dig-ee-tahl-kah-meh-Rah]

dirty schmutzig [shmut-si^{ch}]

discount Ermäßigung, die [eh(r)-may-see-gung]

dish (kind of food) Gericht, das [geh-Ri^{ch}t]

disposable camera Wegwerf-kamera, die [vek-ve(r)f-kah-meh-Rah]

disturb, Do not Bitte nicht stören. [bit-eh ni^{ch}t shter-en]

divorced geschieden [geh-shee-den]

do, to tun [toon]

doctor (male) Artz, der [a(r)tst]; (female) Ärtzin, die [eh(r)t-stin]

dog Hund, der [hoont]

domestic Inland, das [in-lahnt]

done fertig [feh(r)-ti^{ch}]

door Tür, die [tew(r)]

double room Doppelzimmer, das [dop-el-tsim-eh(r)]

download, to herunterladen [heh(r)-un-te(r)-lah-den]

dress Kleid, das [klite]

dried getrocknet [geh-tRok-net]

drink, to trinken [tRink-en]

drinks Getränke, die [geh-tRenk-eh]

drive Fahrt, die [fah(r)t]

driver's license Führerschein, der [fewR-eh(r)-shine]

drugstore Drogerie, die [dRo-geh-Ree]

dry trocken [tRok-en]

dryer Trockner, der [trawk-ne(r)]

duck Ente, die [ent-eh]

dumpling Kloß, der [klos]; Knödel, der [kne(r)-del]

duty (customs/toll) der Zoll [tsol]

ear Ohr, das [oh(r)]

early früh [fRew]

east, to the östlich [erst-li^{ch}]

eat, to essen [es-en]

eat, you du ißt [doo ist] (informal, singular)

eats, he/she/it er/sie/es ißt [ay(r)/zee/es ist]

economical preisgünstig [pRice-gewn-sti^{ch}]

egg Ei, das [eye]

eight acht [ah_{ch}t]

eighteen achtzehn [ah_{ch}t-tsayn]

eighty achtzig [ah_{ch}t-tsi^{ch}]

electricity Strom, der [shtRohm]

elevator Aufzug, der [owf-tsook]

eleven elf [elf]

e-mail E-Mail, die [ee-mayl]

e-mail address E-mail-Adresse, die [ee-mayl-ah-dRess-eh]

end, to enden [end-en]

engineer Ingenieur/-in [in-zheh-new(r)/-in]

England England [eng-lahnt]

English englisch [eng-lish]

enough genug [geh-nook]

entrance (road) Einfahrt, die [ine-fah(r)t]; (building) Eingang, der [ine-gahng]

entry Eintritt, der [ine-tRit]

entry, No Kein Zutritt [kine tsoo-tRit]

envelope Umschlag, der [oom-shlahk]

Euro Euro, der [oy-Roh]

evening Abend, der [ah-bent]

evening, in the abends [ah-bents]

exchange, to wechseln [ve^{ch}-seln]

excursion Ausflug, der [ows-flook]

excuse Entschuldigung, die [ent-shool-dig-ung]

excuse me Entschuldigung [ent-shool-dig-ung]; entschuldigen Sie [ent-shool-dig-en zee]; Verzeihung [feh(r)-tsy-ung]; verzeihen Sie [feh(r)-tsy-en zee]

exercise room Fitnessraum, der [fit-nes-Rowm]

exit (road) Ausfahrt, die [ows-fah(r)t]; (building) Ausgang, der [ows-gahng]

expensive teuer [toy-eh(r)]

eye Auge, das [ow-geh]

eye drops Augentropfen, die [ow-gen-tRop-fen]

Facebook Facebook [fays-book]

Facebook? Are you on Sind Sie auf Facebook? [zint zee owf fays-book?]

facial tissues Taschentücher, die [tah-shen-tew^{ch}-eh(r)]

fall Herbst, der [heh(r)pst]

family Familie, die [fah-meel-yah]

far weit [vite]

farmer Bauer/Bäuerin, der/die [bow-eh(r)/boy-eR-in]

fat fett [fet]

father Vater, der [fah-teh(r)]

Father's Day Vatertag [fah-teh(r)-tahk]

favorable günstig [gewn-sti^{ch}]

fax number Faxnummer, die [fahks-num-e(r)]

feather Feder, die [fay-de(r)]

February Februar [feb-Roo-ah(r)]

fever Fieber, das [fee-beh(r)]

fewer weniger [vay-nig-eh(r)]

field Feld, das [felt]

fifteen fünfzehn [fewnf-tsayn]

fifty fünfzig [fewnf-tsi^{ch}]

fill up the tank, to volltanken [fol-tahnk-en]

film Film, der [film]

finished fertig [feh(r)-ti^{ch}]

fire Feuer, das [foy-eh(r)]

fire department Feuerwehr, die [foy-eh(r)-vay(r)]

fish Fisch, der [fish]

fish dish Fischgericht, das [fish-geh-Ri^{ch}t]

fitness room Fitnessraum, der [fit-nes-Rowm]

five fünf [fewnf]

fix, to reparieren [Rep-ah-ReeR-en]

fixed-price meal Menü, das [meh-new]

flash drive USB-Stick, der [oo-es-bay-stik]

flashlight Taschenlampe, die [tahsh-en-lahm-peh]

flat tire Reifepanne, die [Ry-feh-pah-neh]

flight Flug, der [flook]

floor (of room) Boden, der [boh-den]; (of building) Etage, die [ay-tah-zheh]

flower Blume, die [bloo-meh]

foggy neblig [nay-bli^{ch}]

foot Fuß, der [foos]

for für [few(r)]

forbidden verboten [feh(r)-boh-ten]

foreign lands Ausland, das [ows-lahnt]

fork Gabel, die [gah-bel]

fortress Festung, die [fest-ung]

forty vierzig [fee(r)-tsi^{ch}]

four vier [fee(r)]

fourteen vierzehn [fee(r)-tsayn]

fowl Geflügel, das [geh-flew-gehl]

fragile zerbrechlich [tseh(r)-bRe^{ch} -li^{ch}]

France Frankreich [fRahnk-Ry^{ch}]

French fries Pommes frites, die [pom fRit]

fresh frisch [fRish]

Friday Freitag [fRy-tahk]

friend (male) Freund, der [fRoynt]; (female) Freundin, die [fRoyn-din]

from aus [ows]; von [fon]

from. . . to von. . .bis [fon. . . bis]

frozen eingefroren [ine-geh-fRoh-Ren]

fruit Obst, das [ohpst]

full (booked up) ausgebucht [ows-geh-boo_{ch}t]

furnished möbliert [mer-blee(r)t]

game, wild wild [vilt]

garden Garten, der [gah(r)-ten]

gasoline Benzin, das [ben-tseen]

gas station Tankstelle, die [tahnk-shtel-eh]

gay schwul [shvool]

gentleman Herr, der [hay(r)]

German mark DM, deutsche Mark [doy-cheh mah(r)k]

Germany Deutschland [doych-lahnt]

girl Mädchen, das [mayd-^{ch}en]

girlfriend Freundin, die [fRoyn-din]

glass Glas, das [glahs]
glasses Brille, die [bRil-eh] (singular)
glove Handschuh, der [hahnt-shoo]
gluten Gluten [gloo-ten]
gluten-free glutenfrei [gloo-ten-fRy]
go gehen [gay-en]
"go, to" (food) zum Mitnehmen [tsoom mit-nay-men]
God Gott, der [got]
golden golden [gol-den]
good gut [goot]
goodbye Auf Wiedersehen [owf vee-eh(r)-zayn]; Auf Wiederschauen [owf vee-deh(r)-shau-en]
goose Gans, die [gahns]
goulash Gulasch, das [goo-lahsh]
goulash soup Gulaschsuppe, die [goo-lahsh-zup-eh]
GPS navigator Navi-System, das [nah-vee-zew-staym]
grandchildren Enkel, die [enk-el]
granddaughter Enkelin, die [enk-el-in]
grandfather Großvater, der [gRohs-fah-teh(r)]
grandma Oma, die [oh-mah]
grandmother Großmutter, die [gRohs-mut-eh(r)]
grandpa Opa, der [oh-pah]
grandparents Großeltern, die [gRohs-el-teh(r)n]
grandson Enkel, der [enk-el]
grape Traube, die [tRow-beh]
grass Gras, das [gRahs]
gray grau [gRau]
green grün [gRewn]
greet, to grüßen [gRew-sen]
grilled gegrillt [geh-gRilt]
guesthouse Pension, die [pen-zyohn]
had, he/she/it er/sie/es hatte [ay(r)/zee/es hah-teh]
had, I ich hatte [ich hah-teh]
had, we wir hatten [vee(r) hah-ten]
had, you Sie hatten [zee hah-ten] (formal); du hattest [doo hah-test] (informal, sing.)
hail, to (weather) hageln [hah-geln]
hairdresser (male) Friseur, der [fRi-zew(r)]; (female) Friseuse, die [fRi-zews]
Halloween Halloween
ham Schinken, der [shink-en]

hand Hand, die [hahnt]
handbag Handtasche, die [hahnt-tash-eh]
happy glücklich [glewk-li^ch]
has, he/she/it er/sie/es hat [ay(r)/zee/es haht]
hat Hut, der [hoot]
have, to haben [hah-ben]
have, you Sie haben [zee hah-ben] (formal); du hast [doo hahst] (informal, sing.)
hazelnuts Haselnüsse, die [hah-zel-news-eh]
he er e[eh(r)]
head Kopf, der [kopf]
headache Kopfschmerzen, die [kopf-shmeh(r)t-sen]
headphones Kopfhörer, der [kopf-heR-eh(r)]
health Gesundheit, die [geh-zunt-hite]
health!, To your Zum Wohl! [tsoom vohl]
healthy gesund [geh-zunt]
heart Herz, das [heh(r)ts]
heater Heizgerät, das [hites-geh-Rayt]
hello Guten Morgen/Tag/Abend [goo-ten moh(r)-gen/tahk/ah-bent] (Germ.); Grüß Gott! [gRews got] (Aust.); servus [zeh(r)-voos] (Aust.)
help Hilfe, die [hil-feh]
help, I ich helfe [i^ch hel-feh]
help, to helfen [hel-fen]
help, we wir helfen [vee(r) hel-fen]
help, you Sie helfen [zee hel-fen] (formal); du hilfst [doo hilfst] (informal, singular)
helps, he/she/it er/sie/es hilft [ay(r)/zee/es hilft]
here hier [hee(r)]
high hoch [hohch]
high chair Kinderstuhl, der [kin-deh(r)-shtool]
hill Hügel, der [hew-gehl]
him ihn [een] (acc.); ihm [eem] (dat.)
home country Inland, das [in-lahnt]
honey Honig, der [hoh-ni^ch]
hospital Krankenhaus, das [kRahnk-en-hows]
hot heiß [hice]
hot dog Frankfurter, die [fRahnk-fu(r)-teh(r)]; Wiener Würstchen, das [vee-neh(r) ve(r)st-^ch en]; Hotdog, der [hot-

dok] (includes bun); Würstel, das [ve(r)st-el]

hotel Hotel, das [hoh-tel]; Gasthaus, das [gahst-hows]

hour Stunde, die [shtun-deh]

how wie [vee]

how long wie lange [vee lahng-eh]

how many wie viele [vee fee-leh]

how much wieviel [vee-feel]

hundred hundert [hun-deh(r)t]

hurt weh [vay]

husband (Ehe)Mann, der [(ay-eh)-mahn]

I ich [i^ch]

ice Eis, das [ice]

ice cream Eis, das [ice]

ice cream shop/parlor Eiscafé, das [ice-kah-fay]; Eisdiele, die [ice-dee-leh]; Eissalon, der [ice-sah-lohn]

ice cubes Eiswürfel, die [ice-ve(r)-fel]

identification (card) Ausweis, der [ows-vice]

in in [in]

included inklusive [in-kloo-seev]; inbegriffen [in-beh-gRif-en]

information Auskunft, die [ows-kunft]

inn Gasthaus, das [gahst-hows]

insurance Versicherung, die [feh(r)-zi^ch-eh(r)-ung]

Internet Internet, das [in-teh(r)-net]

Internet, wireless WLAN [vay-lahn]

Internet café Internet Café, das [in-teh(r)-net kah-fay]

iPhone iPhone, der [eye-fone]

iPod iPod, der [eye-pawd]

is, he/she/it er/sie/es ist [ay(r)/zee/es ist]

is, there es gibt [es geept]

Is there ___? Gipt es ___? [geept es ___?]

it es [es]

Italy Italien [ee-tahl-yen]

jacket Jacke, die [yah-keh]

jam Marmelade, die [mah(r)-may-lah-deh]

January Januar [yah-noo-ah(r)]

jaw Kiefer, der [kee-feh(r)]

jeans Jeans, die [jeenz]

juice Saft, der [zahft]

July Juli [yoo-lee]

June Juni [yoo-nee]

ketchup Ketchup, der [ket-chup]

key Schlüssel, der [shlew-sel]

Kleenex Taschentücher, die [tash-en-tew-^ch eh(r)]

knee Knie, das [k-nee]

knife Messer, das [mes-eh(r)]

laborer Arbeiter/-in, der/die [ah(r)-by-teh(r)/-in]

lady Dame, die [dah-meh]

lake See, der [zay]

lamp Lampe, die [lahm-peh]

laptop (computer) Laptop, der [lehp-top]

late spät [shpate]

lawyer Rechtsanwalt/-anwältin, der/die [Re^chts-ahn-vahlt/ahn-velt-tin]

left links [links]

leg Bein, das [bine]

lemon Zitrone, die [tsi-tRohn-eh]

lesbian lesbisch [lez-bish]

less weniger [vay-nig-eh(r)]

letter Brief, der [bReef]

life jacket Schwimmweste, die [shvim-ves-teh]

light (fixture) Licht, das [li^ch t]; (brightness) hell [hel]

light-colored beer, a ein Helles [ine hel-es]

like to gern [geh(r)n]

liter Liter, der [lee-teh(r)]

liter of beer Maß, die [mahs]

little klein [kline]

little, a ein bißchen [ine bis-^ch en]; ein wenig [ine vay-ni^ch]

liver Leber, die [lay-beh(r)]

liver-dumpling soup Leberknödelsuppe, die [lay-beh(r)-kner-del-zup-eh]

local phone call Ortsgespräch, das [oh(r)ts-geh-spRech]

locked out ausgesperrt [ows-geh-shpeh(r)t]

locker Schließfach, das [shlees-fah_ch]

log on, to einloggen [ine-log-en]

log on? How do I Wie logge ich mich ein? [vee log-eh i^ch mi^ch ine?]

long lang [lahng]

long, how wie lange [vee lahng-eh]

look, to schauen [shau-en]

look for, to suchen [zoo-_ch en]

Look out! Vorsicht! [foh(r)-zi^ch t]

lost verloren [feh(r)-loh(r)-en]
loud laut [lowt]
louder, more loudly lauter [lowt-eh(r)]
luggage Gepäck, das [geh-pek]
luggage checkroom
  Gepäckaufbewahrung, die [geh-pek-owf-beh-vahR-ung]
luggage locker Gepäck-schließfach, das [geh-pek-shlees-fah$_{ch}$]
lunch Mittagessen, das [mit-ahg-es-en]
lung Lunge, die [lung-eh]
magazine Zeitschrift, die [tsite-shRift]
mail Post, die [post]
mailbox Briefkasten, der [bReef-kahs-ten]
main course Hauptgericht, das [howpt-geh-Ri^{ch}t]
main square Hauptplatz, der [howpt-plahts]
man Mann, der [mahn]
manager Leiter/-in, der/die [ly-teh(r)/-in]
many viele [fee-leh]
many, too zu viele [tsoo fee-leh]
map Landkarte, die [lahnt-kah(r)-teh]; (city map) Stadtplan, der [shtaht-plahn]
March März [meh(r)ts]
mark (unit of money) Mark, die [mah(r)k]
market Markt, der [mah(r)kt]
married verheiratet [feh(r)-hy-Rah-tet]
May Mai [my]
mayonnaise Mayonnaise, die [my-oh-nay-zeh]
me mich (dir. obj.) [mi^{ch}]
me, for für mich [few(r) mi^{ch}]
meadow Wiese, die [vee-zeh]
meat Fleisch, das [flysh]
meat dish Fleischgericht, das [flysh-geh-Ri^{ch}t]
meat patty Frikadelle, die [fRik-ah-del-eh]
meat roll Roulade, die [Roo-lah-deh]
mechanic Mechaniker/-in [meh-^{ch}ah-nee-keh(r)/-in]
medication Medikament, das [meh-dee-kah-ment]
medicine Medikament, das [meh-dee-kah-ment]

medium (meat) mittel [mit-el]; halb-durch [hahlp-du(r)$_{ch}$]
memory card Speicherkarte, die [shpy-^{ch}eh(r)-kah(r)-teh]
memory stick USB-Stick, der [oo-es-bay-stik]
menu Speisekarte, die [shpy-zeh-kah(r)-teh]
merge, traffic Reißverschluss, der [Rys-feh(r)-shlus]
message (e.g., note) Nachricht, die [nah$_{ch}$-Ri^{ch}t]
microphone Mikrofon, das [mee-kRoh-fohn]
middle Mitte, die [mit-eh]
midnight Mitternacht, die [mit-eh(r)-nah$_{ch}$t]
milk Milch, die [mil^{ch}]
milk products Milchprodukte, die [mil^{ch}-pRoh-duk-teh]
million Million, die [mil-yohn]
mineral water Mineralwasser, das [min-eh(r)-ahl-wahs-eh(r)]
minister Pfarrer/-in, der/die [pfah-Reh(r)/-in]
minus minus [mee-nus]
minute Minute, die [mi-noo-teh]
miss Fräulein, das [fRoy-line]
mixed gemischt [geh-misht]
moment Moment, der [moh-ment]
Monday Montag [mohn-tahk]
money Geld, das [gelt]
month Monat, der [mohn-aht]
more mehr [may(r)]
morning (early) Morgen, der [mo(r)-gen]; (mid- and late) Vormittag, der [foh(r)-mit-tahk]
morning, in the morgens [mo(r)-gens]
mosquito Mücke, die [mew-keh]; Gelse, die [gehl-seh] (Aust.)
mother Mutter, die [mut-eh(r)]
Mother's Day Muttertag [mut-eh(r)-tahk]
motorcycle Motorrad, das [moh-to(r)-Raht]
mountain Berg, der [be(r)k]
mouth Mund, der [munt]
MP3 player MP3-Player, der [em-pay-dRy-play-e(r)]
MSG (Mono)natriumglutamat, das [(moh-noh) nah-tree-oom-gloo-tah-maht]

much viel [feel]
much, too zu viel [tsoo feel]
mug Becher, der [be^{ch}-eh(r)]
muscle Muskel, der [mus-kel]
museum Museum, das [mu-zay-um]
mushroom Pilz, der [pilts]
musician Musiker/-in, der/die [moo-zee-keh(r)/-in]
mustard Senf, der [zenf]
my mein [mine]
name Name, der [nah-meh]
napkin Serviette, die [zeh(r)-vyet-eh]
nearby in der Nähe [in day(r) nay-eh]
neck Hals, der [hahls]
necktie Krawatte, die [kRah-vah-teh]
need brauchen [bRow-chen]
nephew Neffe, der [nef-eh]
network Netz, das [nets]
newspaper Zeitung, die [tsy-tung]
nice schön [shern]
niece Nichte, die [ni^{ch}-teh]
night Nacht, die [nah_{ch}t]
nine neun [noyn]
nineteen neunzehn [noyn-tsayn]
ninety neunzig [noyn-tsi^{ch}]
no nein [nine]
no/none kein/e [kine/ky-neh]
noisy laut [lowt]
non-alcoholic beer alkoholfreies Bier [ahl-koh-hohl-fRy-es bee(r)]
non-carbonated still [shtil]
noodle Nudel, die [noo-del]
noon Mittag, der [mit-ahk]
north, to the nördlich [nerd-li^{ch}]
nose Nase, die [nah-zeh]
nose drops Nasentropfen, die [nah-zeh-tRop-fen]
nose spray Nasenspray, das [nah-zen-shpRay]
not nicht [ni^{ch}t]
nothing nichts [ni^{ch}ts]
nothing, It's Es macht nichts. [es mah_{ch}t ni^{ch}ts]
November November [noh-vem-beh(r)]
nude beach designation FKK [eff-kah-kah]
number Zahl, die [tsahl]
nun Nonne, die [non-eh]
nurse (female) Krankenschwester, die [kRahnk-en-shvest-eh(r)]; (male)

Krankenpfleger, der [kRahnk-en-pflay-geh(r)]
nuts Nüsse, die [new-seh]
occupation Beruf, der [beh-Roof]
occupied besetzt [beh-zetst]
October Oktober [ok-toh-beh(r)]
oil Öl, das [erl]
old city Altstadt, die [ahlt-shtaht]
omelet Omelett, das [om-let]
on auf [owf]
one eins [ines]
one-way (ticket) einfach [ine-fa^{ch}]
one-way street Einbahn-straße, die [ine-bahn-shtRah-seh]
onion Zwiebel, die [tvee-bel]
onion soup Zwiebelsuppe, die [tvee-bel-zup-eh]
only nur [noo(r)]
open(ed) geöffnet [geh-erf-net]
optometrist Augenoptiker, der [ow-gehn-op-tee-keh(r)]
or oder [oh-deh(r)]
orange (color) orange [oh-Rahn-zheh]; (fruit) Orange, die [oh-Rahn-zheh], Apfelsine, die [ahp-fel-zee-neh]
order, to place an bestellen [beh-shtel-en]
organic Bio [bee-oh]; organisch [oh(r)-gahn-ish]
organic products Bioprodukte, die [bee-oh-pRoh-duk-teh]
outside draußen [dRow-zen]
over (location) über [ew-beh(r)]
overcoat Mantel, der [mahn-tel]
overdrawn überzogen [ew-beh(r)-tsohg-en]
pacifier (baby) Schnuller, der [shnul-eh(r)]
package Paket, das [pah-kate]
packaging Verpackung, die [feh(r)-pah-kung]
palace Schloß, das [shlos]; Palast, der [pah-lahst]
pants, pair of Hose, die [hoh-zeh]
paper Papier, das [pah-pee(r)]
paper, writing Schreibpapier, das [shRipe-pah-pee(r)]
parcel Paket, das [pah-kate]
pardon Verzeihung, die [feh(r)-tsy-ung]
Pardon me! Verzeihung! [feh(r)-tsy-ung]; Pardon! [pah(r)-dohn]

parents Eltern, die [el-teh(r)n]

park Park, der [pah(r)k]

parking, No Parkverbot [pah(r)k-feh(r)-boht]

partner (male) Partner, der [pah(r)t-neh(r)]; (female) Partnerin, die [pah(r)t-nehR-in]

passport Paß, der [pahs]; Reisepaß, der [Ry-zeh-pahs]

passport control Kontrolle, die [kon-tRol-eh]

pastries Gebäck, das [geh-bek]

pastry shop Konditorei, die [kon-dee-tohR-eye]

pay, to bezahlen [beh-tsahl-en]

pay attention Passen Sie auf! [pah-sen zee owf]

peach Pfirsich, der [pfi(r)-zi^ch]

peanuts Erdnüsse, die [eh(r)t-new-seh]

pear Birne, die [bee(r)-neh]

peas Erbsen, die [eh(r)p-sen]

pen, ballpoint Kuli, der [koo-lee]

penicillin Penizillin, das [pen-ee-tsi-leen]

pepper Pfeffer, der [pfef-eh(r)]

person Person, die [peh(r)-zohn]

pet Haustier, das [hows-tee(r)]

pharmacy Apotheke, die [ah-po-tay-keh]

phone card internationale Prepaid-Telefonkarte, die [in-te(r)-naht-see-oh-nah-lay pree-payd teh-leh-fohn-kah(r)-teh]

photoshop Fotogeschäft, das [foh-toh-geh-sheft]

pictures, taking Fotografieren, das [foh-toh-gRah-fee-Ren]

piece Stück, das [stewk]

pillow Kopfkissen, das [kopf-kis-en]

pilot Pilot/-in, der/die [pee-loht/-in]

Pilsner beer Pils, das [pils]

PIN Geheimnummer, die [geh-hime-num-eh(r)]

pineapple Ananas, die [ah-nah-nahs]

pink rosa [Roh-zah]

plant Pflanze, die [pflahn-tseh]

plate Teller, der [tel-eh(r)]

playground Spielplatz, der [shpeel-plahts]

please bitte [bit-eh] (also "bitte bitte" and "bitte schön")

plumber Klempner, der [klemp-neh(r)]

p.m. abends [ah-bents]

police Polizei, die [poh-li-tsy]

pond Teich, der [ty^ch]

pop Limonade, die [lee-moh-nah-deh]

pork Schweinefleisch, das [shvine-eh-flysh]

pork chop Schweinekotelett, das [shvine-eh-kot-let]

portion Portion, die [po(r)-tsyohn]

postage stamp Briefmarke, die [bReef-mah(r)-keh]

postcard Postkarte, die [post-kah(r)-teh]

post office Post, die [post]

potato Kartoffel, die [kah(r)-tof-el]; Erdapfel, der [eh(r)t-ahp-fel] (Aust.)

potty chair Kindertöpchen, das [kin-deh(r)-terp-^chen]

poultry Geflügel, das [geh-flew-gehl]

pregnant schwanger [shvahng-eh(r)]

prepaid card (cell phone) Prepaidkarte, die [pRee-payd-kah(r)-teh]

prescription Rezept, das [Ray-tsept]

press drücken [dRew-ken]

pretty schön [shern]

priest Priester, der [p(r)ee-steh(r)]

printer Drucker, der [dRuk-e(r)]

professor Professor/-in, der/die [pRoh-fes-o(r)/pRoh-fes-oh-Rin]

pub Bierstube, die [bee(r)-shtoo-beh]; Kneipe [kny-peh]

pull, to ziehen [tsee-en]

pullover Pullover, der [pul-oh-veh(r)]

purple violett [vee-oh-let]

purse Handtasche, die [hahnt-tahsh-eh]

push drücken [dRew-ken]

quarter Viertel, der [fee(r)-tel]

quiet leise [ly-zeh]

rain Regen, der [Ray-gen]

rain, to regnen [Rayg-nen]

raining, it's Es regnet [es Rayg-net]

rare (meat) blütig [blew-ti^ch]; englisch [eng-lish]

raspberry Himbeere, die [him-bayR-eh]

rates Gebühren, die [geh-bew-Rehn]

raw roh [Roh]

razor Rasierapparat, der [Rah-<u>zee(r)</u>-ah-pah-Raht]

razor blade Rasierklinge, die [Rah-<u>zee(r)</u>-kling-eh]

ready fertig [<u>feh(r)</u>-ti^{ch}]

receipt Quittung, die [<u>kvit</u>-ung]

recommend, to empfehlen [emp-<u>fay</u>-len]

recycle, to recyceln [Ree-<u>sy</u>-keln]

recycle this? Where can I Wo kann ich das recyceln? [voh kahn i^{ch} dahs Ree-<u>sy</u>-keln?]

red rot [Roht]

red cabbage Blaukraut, das [<u>blau</u>-kRowt]

red wine Rotwein, der [<u>Roht</u>-vine]

refrigerator Kühlschrank, der [<u>kewl</u>-shRahnk]

rent, to mieten [<u>meet</u>-en]

rental car Mietwagen, der [<u>meet</u>-vah-gen]

repeat, to wiederholen [vee-deh(r)-<u>hoh</u>-len]

reservation Reservierung, die [Reh-zeh(r)-<u>veeR</u>-ung]

rest, day of Ruhetag, der [<u>Roo</u>-eh-tahk]

restaurant Gasthaus, das [<u>gahst</u>-hows]; Gaststätte, die [<u>gahst</u>-stet-eh]; das Restaurant [Res-to-<u>Rah</u>]

rest room Toilette, die [toy-<u>let</u>-eh]; WC, das [vay-<u>tsay</u>]

rest stop Raststation, die [<u>Rahst</u>-stah-tsyohn]; Rasthof, der [<u>Rahst</u>-hof]

retired person Rentner/-in, der/die [<u>Rent</u>-neh(r)/-in]

rice Reis, der [Rice]

ride Fahrt, die [fah(r)t]

right rechts [Re^{ch}ts]

river Fluß, der [floos]

roll Brötchen, das [<u>bReht</u>-^{ch}en]; Semmel, die [<u>zem</u>-el] (Aust.); Schrippe, die [<u>shRip</u>-eh] (Berlin)

room Zimmer, das [<u>tsim</u>-eh(r)]

rooster Hahn, der [hahn]

roundabout Kreisverkehr, der [<u>kRys</u>-feh(r)-keh(r)]

round trip hin und zurück [hin unt tsoo-<u>Rewk</u>]

sack Tüte, die [<u>tew</u>-teh]

sad traurig [<u>tRow</u>-Ri^{ch}]

salad Salat, der [zah-<u>laht</u>]

sale Ausverkauf, der [<u>ows</u>-feh(r)-kowf]

salesperson Verkäufer/-in, der/die [feh(r)-<u>koy</u>-feh(r)/-in]

sales representative Vertreter/-in, der/die [feh(r)-<u>tRay</u>-teh(r)/-in]

sales tax Mehrwertsteuer, die [may(r)-vay(r)t-<u>shtoy</u>-eh(r)]

salmon Lachs, der [la_{ch}s]

salt Salz, das [zahlts]

salty salzig [<u>zahlt</u>-si^{ch}]

Saturday Samstag [<u>zahm</u>-stahk]; Sonnabend [<u>zon</u>-ah-bent]

sausage Wurst, die [vu(r)st]

sausage stand Würstelstand, der [<u>vew(r)</u>-stel-shtahnt]

scanner Scanner, der [<u>skeh</u>-ne(r)]

schilling Schilling, der [<u>shil</u>-ing]

schnitzel Schnitzel, das [<u>shnit</u>-sel]

scientist Wissenschaftler/-in, der/die [<u>vis</u>-en-shahft-leh(r)/-in]

scoop (ice cream) Kugel, die [<u>koo</u>-gehl]

scooter Roller, der [<u>Rol</u>-eh(r)]

sea See, der [zay]

seafood Meeresfrüchte, die [<u>mayR</u>-es-fRewk-teh]

seasick seekrank [<u>zay</u>-kRahnk]

seasoning Würze, die [<u>vew(r)t</u>-seh]

second Sekunde, die [zeh-<u>kun</u>-deh]

secretary Sekretär/-in, der/die [zek-Reh-<u>tay(r)</u>/-in]

self-employed person Selbständige, der/die [<u>zelp</u>-shten-dig-eh]

self-service Selbstbedienung, die [<u>zelpst</u>-beh-deen-ung]; SB [es-bay]

separate getrennt [geh-<u>tRent</u>]

September September [zep-<u>tem</u>-beh(r)]

service Bedienung, die [beh-<u>deen</u>-ung]

set-priced meal Menü, das [meh-<u>new</u>]

set-priced meal of the day Tagesmenü, das [<u>tahg</u>-es-meh-new]

seven sieben [<u>zee</u>-ben]

seventeen siebzehn [<u>zeep</u>-tsayn]

seventy siebzig [<u>zeep</u>-tsi^{ch}]

shampoo Shampoo, das [shahm-<u>poo</u>]

shaving cream Rasiercreme, die [Rah-<u>zee(r)</u>-kRem]

she sie [zee]

sheet Bettlaken, das [<u>bet</u>-lah-ken]

shellfish Schaltiere, die [<u>shahl</u>-teeR-eh]

shirt Hemd, das [hemt]

shoe Schuh, der [shoo]

shoulder Schulter, die [shul-teh(r)]

shower Dusche, die [doo-sheh]

shutters (heavy exterior roll-up ones) Rollladen, der [rol-lah-den]

siblings Geschwister, die (pl) [geh-shvis-teh(r)]

sick krank [kRahnk]

side dish Beilage, die [by-lah-geh]

sign, to unterschreiben [oon-te(r)-shribe-en]

silver silbern [zil-beh(r)n]

SIM card SIM-Karte, die [zim-kah(r)-teh]

simple einfach [ine-fa_{ch}]

single (marital status) ledig [lay-di^{ch}]

single room Einzelzimmer, das [ine-tsel-tsim-eh(r)]

sister Schwester, die [shvest-eh(r)]

six sechs [ze^{ch}s]

sixteen sechszehn [ze^{ch}-tsayn]

sixty sechzig [ze^{ch}-tsi^{ch}]

skin Haut, die [howt]

skirt Rock, der [Rok]

Skype Skype [skipe]

sleeping bag Schlafsack, der [shlahf-zahk]

slice, a eine Scheibe [ine-eh shy-beh]

slow, slowly langsam [lahng-zahm]

small klein [kline]

smoked geräuchert [geh-Roy^{ch}-e(r)t]

smoking Rauchen, das [Rau-_{ch}en]

snack Snack, der [snek]

snack bar Schnellimbiß, der [shnel-im-bis]

snow Schnee, der [shnay]

snow, to schneien [shny-en]

snowing, it's Es schneit [es shnite]

soap Seife, die [zy-feh]

sock Socke, die [zok-eh]

soda pop Limonade, die [lee-moh-nah-deh]

soft drink Softdrink, der [soft-dRink]; Limonade, die [lee-moh-nah-deh]

something etwas [et-vahs]

son Sohn, der [zohn]

soup Suppe, die [zup-eh]

soup of the day Tagessuppe, die [tahg-es-zup-eh]

sour sauer [zow-eh(r)]

south, to the südlich [zewd-li^{ch}]

Spain Spanien [shpahn-yen]

sparkling (water, wine) prickelnd [prik-elnd]; sprudelnd [shpRood-elnd]

speak, I ich spreche [i^{ch} shpRe^{ch}-eh]

speak, to sprechen [shpRe^{ch}-en]

speak, you Sie sprechen [zee spRe^{ch}-en] (formal); du sprichst [doo shpRi^{ch}st] (informal, singular)

speaks, he/she/it er/sie/es spricht [ayr/zee/es shpRi^{ch}t]

special, day's (meal) Tagesmenü, das [tahg-es-meh-new] (meal)

special offer Sonderangebot, das [zon-deh(r)-ahn-geh-boht]

specialty Spezialität, die [shpet-see-ah-lee-tate]

speciality of the house Hausspezialität, die [hows-shpet-see-ah-lee-tate]

spoon Löffel, der [lerf-el]

spring Frühling, der [fRew-ling]

square, main Hauptplatz, der [howpt-plahts]

stamp Briefmarke, die [bReef-mah(r)-keh]

steak Steak, das [stake]

steamed gedämpft [geh-dempft]

stew Eintopf, der [ine-topf]

sticker, traffic toll Vignette, die [vin-yet]

stolen gestohlen [geh-shtoh-len]

stomach Magen, der [mah-gen]

stomach pains Magenschmerzen, die [mah-gen-shmeh(r)t-sen]

stop (noun) Halt, der [halt]

Stop! Halten Sie! [halt-en zee]

stop, to halten [halt-en]

story (of building) Etage, die [ay-tah-zheh]

straight ahead geradeaus [geh-Rah-deh-ows]

strawberry Erdbeere, die [eh(r)t-bayR-eh]

streetcar Straßenbahn, die [shtRah-sen-bahn]

stroller (child's) Kinderwagen, der [kin-deh(r)-vahg-en]

student Student/-in, der/die [shtoo-dent/-in]

suburban train S-Bahn, die [es-bahn]

subway U-Bahn, die [oo-bahn]

sugar Zucker, der [tsuk-eh(r)]

suitcase Koffer, der [k**of**-eh(r)]
summer Sommer, der [z**om**-eh(r)]
Sunday Sonntag [z**on**-tahk]
sunglasses Sonnenbrille, die [z**on**-en-bR**i**l-eh] (singular)
sunny sonnig [z**on**-i^ch^]
suntan lotion Sonnencreme, die [z**on**-en-kRem]
suntan oil Sonnenöl, das [z**on**-en-erl]
supermarket Supermarkt, der [z**oo**-peh(r)-mah(r)kt]
supper Abendessen, das [**ah**-bent-es-en]
supper of open-faced sandwiches Abendbrot, das [**ah**-bent-bRoht]
sweater Pullover, der [pul-**oh**-veh(r)]
sweet süß [zews]; (candy) Süßigkeit, das [z**ews**-i^ch^-keit]; (candy) Bonbon, der [bon-**bon**]
sweetener, artificial Süßstoff, der [z**ews**-shtof]
swimming pool Schwimmbad, das [s**hvim**-baht]
swim suit Badeanzug, der [b**ah**-deh-ahn-tsook]
swim trunks Badehose, die [b**ah**-deh-hoh-zeh]
Switzerland die Schweiz [shvyts]
table Tisch, der [tish]
take, to nehmen [n**ay**-men]
take it (not), I'll Ich nehme es (nicht). [i^ch^ n**ay**-meh es (ni^ch^t)]
take-out/take-away (food) zum Mitnehmen [tsoom m**it**-nay-men]
tap water Leitungswasser, das [l**y**-tungs-wah-seh(r)]
taste, to schmecken [s**hmek**-en]
tastes good, it Es schmeckt (gut)! [es shmekt (goot)]
tax Steuer, die [s**htoy**-eh(r)]
taxi Taxi, das [t**ahk**-see]
tea Tee, der [tay]
teacher Lehrer/-in, der/die [l**ayR**-eh(r)/-in]
telephone Telefon, das [t**eh**-leh-fohn]
ten zehn [tsayn]
tent Zelt, das [tselt]
terrible schrecklich [s**hRek**-li^ch^]
thank you danke [d**ahnk**-eh] (also "Danke schön," "Danke vielmals" and "Vielen Dank")
that das [dahs]

there da [dah]; dort [do(r)t]
there and back hin und zurück [hin unt tsoo-R**ewk**]
there are es gibt [es geept]
there is es gibt [es geept]
thing Ding, das [ding]
thirteen dreizehn [dR**y**-tsayn]
thirty dreißig [dR**y**-si^ch^]
thousand tausend [t**ow**-zent]
three drei [dRy]
throat Hals, der [hahls]
thumb drive USB-Stick, der [oo-es-b**ay**-stik]
Thursday Donnerstag [d**on**-eh(r)s-tahk]
ticket Karte, die [k**ahR**-teh]; (transportation) Fahrkarte, die [f**ah**(r)-kah(r)-teh]; (admission) Eintrittskarte, die [**ine**-tRits-kah(r)-teh]
ticket, child's (transportation) Kinderfahrkarte, die [k**in**-deh(r)-f**ah**(r)-kah(r)-teh]
ticket, day Tageskarte, die [t**ahg**-es-kah(r)-teh]
ticket, week Wochenkarte, die [v**oh**ch-en-kah(r)-teh]
time Zeit, die [tsite]
tire Reifen, der [R**y**-fen]
tired müde [m**ew**-deh]
to (duration) bis [bis]; (clock time) vor [foh(r)]; (destination) nach [nahch] or zu [tsoo]; (allergic) gegen [g**ay**-gen]
"to go" (food) zum Mitnehmen [tsoom m**it**-nay-men]
toast Toast, der [tohst]
tobacconist's shop Tabakhandlung [tah-b**ahk**-hahnt-lung] (Germ.); Tabaktrafik, die [tah-b**ahk**-tRah-feek] (Aust.)
today heute [h**oy**-teh]
together zusammen [tsoo-z**ah**-men]
toilet Toilette, die [toy-l**et**-eh]
toilet paper Toilettenpapier, das [toy-let-en-pah-pee(r)]
toll (customs/duty) Zoll, der [tsol]; (highway) Maut, die [mowt]
toll sticker (for highway toll) Vignette, die [vin-y**et**]
tomato Tomate, die [toh-m**ah**-teh]
tomato soup Tomatensuppe, die [toh-m**ah**-ten-zup-eh]

tomorrow morgen [mohʀ-gen]
tonsils Mandeln, die [mahn-deln]
too zu [tsoo]
too many zu viele [tsoo fee-leh]
too much zu viel [tsoo feel]
tooth Zahn, der [tsahn]
toothpaste Zahnpasta, die [tsahn-pahs-tah]
torte Torte, die [toh(r)-teh]
touch berühren [be-ʀewʀ-en]
touch!, Don't Nicht berühren! [ni^ch t be-ʀewʀ-en]
tough zäh [tsay]
tourist information Touristeninformation, die [too-ʀis-ten-in-fo(r)-mah-tsyohn]
towel (small) Handtuch, das [hahnt-too_ch]; (large) Badetuch, das [bah-deh-too_ch]
town hall Rathaus, das [ʀaht-hows]
toy Spielzeug, das [shpeel-tsoyk]
trade fair Messe, die [mes-eh]
traffic jam Stau, der [shtow]
traffic merge Reißverschluss, der [ʀys-feh(r)-shlus]
train Zug, der [tsook]
train, city and suburban S-Bahn, die [es-bahn]
train platform Bahnsteig, der [bahn-shtike]
train station Bahnhof, der [bahn-hof]
train station, main Hauptbahnhof, der [howpt-bahn-hof]
train ticket Fahrkarte, die [fah(r)-kah(r)-teh]
train track Gleis, das [glice]
trash can Abfalleimer [ahp-fahl-ime-eh(r)]
traveler's check Reisescheck, der [ʀy-zeh-shek]
tree Baum, der [bowm]
trip Fahrt, die [fah(r)t]; Reise, die [ʀy-zeh]
trout Forelle, die [foh(r)-el-eh]
try on, to anprobieren [ahn-pʀoh-beeʀ-en]
T-shirt T-Shirt, das [tee-shi(r)t]
Tuesday Dienstag [deens-tahk]
tuna Thunfisch, der [toon-fish]
turkey Truthahn, der [tʀoot-hahn]
twelve zwölf [tsverlf]
twenty zwanzig [tsvahn-tsi^ch]

two zwei [tsvy]; zwo [tsvoh]
umbrella Regenschirm, der [ʀay-gen-shi(r)m]
uncle Onkel, der [onk-el]
under unten [un-ten]
underclothes Unterwäsche, die [un-teh(r)-vesh-eh]
understand, to verstehen [feh(r)-shtay-en]
underwear, pair of Unterhose, die [un-teh(r)-hoh-zeh]
unemployed arbeitslos [ah(r)-bites-lohs]
United States, the Vereinigten Staaten, die [feh(r)-eye-nik-ten shtah-ten]
until bis [bis]
up auf [owf]
upon auf [owf]
USA die USA [oo-es-ah]
USB flash drive USB-Stick, der [oo-es-bay-stik]
use, to benutzen [beh-nuht-tsen]
vacant frei [fʀy]
vacation apartment Ferienwohnung, die [feh(r)-ee-en-voh-nung]
Valentine's Day Valentinstag [vah-len-teens-tahk]
veal Kalbfleisch, das [kahlp-flysh]
vegetables Gemüse, das [geh-mew-zeh]
vegetarian vegetarisch [vay-gay-tahʀ-ish]
vegetarian food vegetarisches Essen [vay-gay-tahʀ-ish-es es-en]
vinegar Essig, der [es-i^ch]
waiter Kellner, der [kel-neh(r)]
waitress Kellnerin, die [kel-neh(r)-in]
walker (med.) Gehwagen, der [gay-vahg-en]
walking stick Gehstock, der [gay-shtock]
wall Wand, die [vahnt]
warm warm [vah(r)m]
was, I/he/she/it ich/er/sie/es war [i^ch /ay(r)/zee/es vah(r)]
washing machine Waschmachine, die [vahsh-mah-shee-neh]
waste, non-recyclable Restmüll, der [ʀest-mewl]
wastebasket Papierkorb, der [pah-pee(r)-ko(r)p]

Watch out! Passen Sie auf! [pah-sen
  zee owf]; Vorsicht! [foh(r)-zi^{ch}t]
water Wasser, das [vah-seh(r)]
water closet WC, das [vay-tsay]
water, tap Leitungswasser, das [ly-
  tungs-vah-seh(r)]
we wir [vee(r)]
weak schwach [shvah$_{ch}$]
weather Wetter, das [vet-eh(r)]
Wednesday Mittwoch [mit-vo$_{ch}$]
week Woche, die [vo$_{ch}$-eh]
weekend Wochenende, das [vo$_{ch}$-en-
  end-eh]
week ticket Wochenkarte, die [voh$_{ch}$-
  en-kah(r)-teh]
well gut [goot]
well-done (meat) gut durchgebraten
  [goot du(r)^{ch}-geh-bRah-ten]
were, you Sie waren [zee vahR-en]
  (formal); du warst [doo vah(r)st]
  (informal, singular)
were, we wir waren [vee(r) vahR-en]
west, to the westlich [vest-li^{ch}]
wet wipes feuchte Tücher [foy$_{ch}$-teh
  tew^{ch}-e(r)]
what was [vahs]
wheel Rad, das [Raht]
wheelchair Rollstuhl, der [Rol-shtewl]
when wann [vahn]
where wo [voh]
where from woher [voh-hay(r)]
where to wohin [voh-hin]
whipped cream Schlagsahne, die
  [shlahk-zah-neh]; Schlagobers, das
  [shlahk-oh-beh(r)s]; Schlagrahm, der
  [shlahk-Rahm]
white weiß [vice]
white wine Weißwein, der [vice-vine]
who wer [vay(r)]
why warum [vah-Room]
wife Frau, die [fRow]
wifi Wi-Fi [vee-fee]
window Fenster, das [fen-steh(r)]

window seat Fensterplatz, der [fen-
  ste(r)-plahts]
windy windig [vin-di^{ch}]
wine Wein, der [vine]
wine list Weinliste, die [vine-list-eh]
winter Winter, der [vin-teh(r)]
wipes, wet feuchte Tücher [foy$_{ch}$-teh
  tew^{ch}-e(r)]
wireless Internet WLAN [vay-lahn]
with mit [mit]
without ohne [oh-neh]
woman Frau, die [fRow]
would like to möchten [mer^{ch}-ten]
would like to, I/he/she/it
  ich/er/sie/es möchte [i^{ch}/ay(r)/zee/
  es mer^{ch}-teh]
would like to, you Sie möchten [zee
  mer^{ch}-ten] (formal); du möchtest
  [doo mer^{ch}-test] (informal, singular)
wristwatch Armbanduhr, die
  [ah(r)m-bahnt-oo(r)]
writer Schriftsteller/-in, der/die
  [shRift-shtel-eh(r)/-in]
writing paper Schreibpapier, das
  [shRipe-pah-pee(r)]
yard Garten, der [gah(r)-ten]
year Jahr, das [yah(r)]
yellow gelb [gelp]
yes ja [yah]
yesterday gestern [ges-teh(r)n]
yogurt Joghurt, der [yoh-gu(r)t]
you Sie [zee] (formal); du [doo]
  (informal, singular)
you, for für Sie (dir. obj.) [few(r) zee]
youth hostel Jugendherberge, die
  [yoog-ent-heh(r)-beh(r)-geh]
zero null [nul]
zip code Postleitzahl, die [post-lite-
  tsahl]
zipper Reißverschluss, der [Rys-feh(r)-
  shlus]

Index

Other Books by Elizabeth Bingham

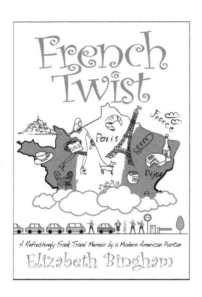

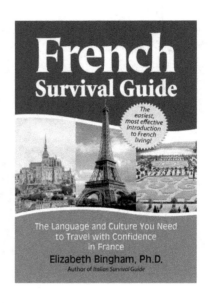

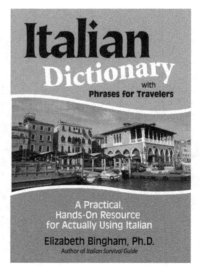

CPSIA information can be obtained
at www.ICGtesting.com
Printed in the USA
LVHW031455050619
620258LV00014B/817/P

9 780970 373465